CORONA VIRUS

COVID-19

FACT OR FICTION?

YOU DECIDE

Published 2020: Golden Child Promotions Publishing Ltd

Portland House,

Belmont Business Park,

Durham,

DH1 1TW

9x9x9@goldenchildpromotionspublishing.com

Coronavirus: Covid-19 Fact Or Fiction? You Decide

Read This First! Download CHOICES! Natural Order vs Unnatural Order!
Ebook FREE!

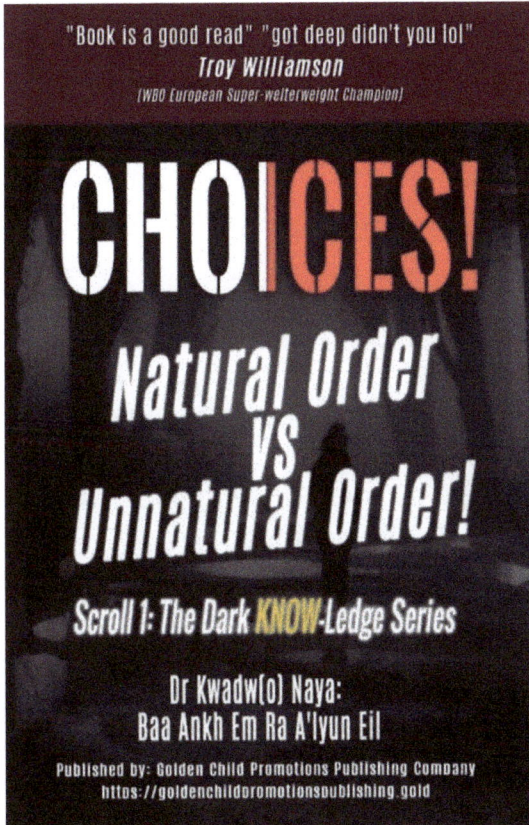

Just to say thanks for purchasing this book, I would like to give you this e-book worth $6.99 for free! Just click on the link below and it's all yours.

https://BookHip.com/FJVSKH

Hi, ladies and gentleman. I hope you are well! I really didn't want to speak about or comment on this topic but someone has to.

What in the world is going on!?

A lot of people are confused out there. That's why I had to do some digging and my findings are rather interesting. Come with me as I unravel the truth behind all these which, by the way, is going to blow your mind.

But before that, let me introduce myself:

My name is Dr Kwadwo Naya: Baa Ankh Em Ra Alyun Eil. I live in Darlington in the North East of England (UK) and my business is registered in Durham. I am an author and publisher with 21 books to my name till date. This book will be my 22nd or 23rd.

I run the publishing company 'Golden Child Promotions Publishing Ltd', a book publishing company which is committed to giving all quality voices a chance. At Golden Child Promotions Publishing, we assist authors or aspiring authors to publish their works for minimum cost, with the author retaining all royalties and profit. We do this by bridging the space between the various medium of publishing and offer quality opportunities to gifted writers who have never been able to express their thoughts or have their works published as a result of the short-handedness of traditional publishing.

When you get the opportunity, kindly check out our website goldenchildpromotionspublishing.gold and you will see the proof of the pudding. We have many great books available and upcoming and a lot of great talent coming through the ranks both big and small, please stay tuned.

As I was saying, I didn't really want to comment on this subject, epidemic, pandemic – whatever you want to call it. But the situation is getting out of hand. Someone needs to speak out. So here we are.

Source: [1]

Which house do you live in?

1   https://www.facebook.com/photo.php?fbid=102955
    8440778982&set=a.1062205 09779451&type=3&theater
    accessed April 19th 2020 @19:15

CONTENTS

Failure to carry your umbrella after hearing a forecast of heavy rain makes for a baseless complaint when you are soaking wet. 🎋□

Two Things: - Don't let this be you - Don't miss this message – Kurtis Tompkins

INTRODUCTION

With ground-breaking technological advancements, you would think that events such as a pandemic have no right to cripple and bring the world to its knees. I am sure nobody envisaged this on New Year's Eve But it has happened. People have now raised eyebrows. Questions are being asked.

Is the virus **REAL**, **NATURAL** or **FAKE** and **MANUFACTURED?**

Very good questions if you ask me.

Let us go for a history class:

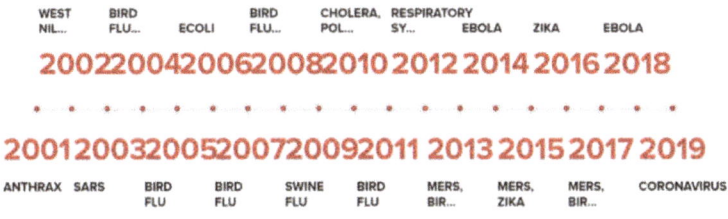

WEST NIL...	BIRD FLU...	ECOLI	BIRD FLU...	CHOLERA, POL...	RESPIRATORY SY...	EBOLA	ZIKA	EBOLA
2002	2004	2006	2008	2010	2012	2014	2016	2018

2001	2003	2005	2007	2009	2011	2013	2015	2017	2019
ANTHRAX	SARS	BIRD FLU	BIRD FLU	SWINE FLU	BIRD FLU	MERS, BIR...	MERS, ZIKA	MERS, BIR...	CORONAVIRUS

---

2 https://www.who.int/csr/don/archive/year/en/ accessed March 18th 2020 @14:12

(1)

Every year there seems to be an epidemic which spreads fear among nations. It is more than a coincidence if you ask me. It makes one wonder if these anomalies have been planned, manufactured, and executed with a motive in mind? Or if they are a result of natural sources or our own neglect?

We have a pandemic on our hands. Coronavirus is with US now and this is the BIG NEWS... **MOST OF US KNOW!** BUT this VIRUS in question, this supposed viral pneumonia has had more hype surrounding it than the black plague ever did. But when you observe closely, you will find out that things are not as they seem.

This BLACK PLAQUE like DISEASE does not seem as bad as it is hyped. Let us look at some figures: Considering that coronavirus has a contagion factor of 2, whereas SARS is 4 and measles is 18, things would be far worse if everyone had measles.

Coronavirus has a cure rate of 99.7% for those under 50. This does not seem so bad after all. But the MEDIA appear to have it ALL WRONG. The NAÏVE TRUSTING SLAVES are allowing the MEDIA to CONTROL their MINDS. But, I am sure you are that naïve to reframe from asking questions.

THEY say that coronavirus is a new virus, but the truth is, it has been prevalent in animals for years, such to the extent that they have been vaccinating the animals. Do not just take my word for it, check it out for yourself and you will SEE.

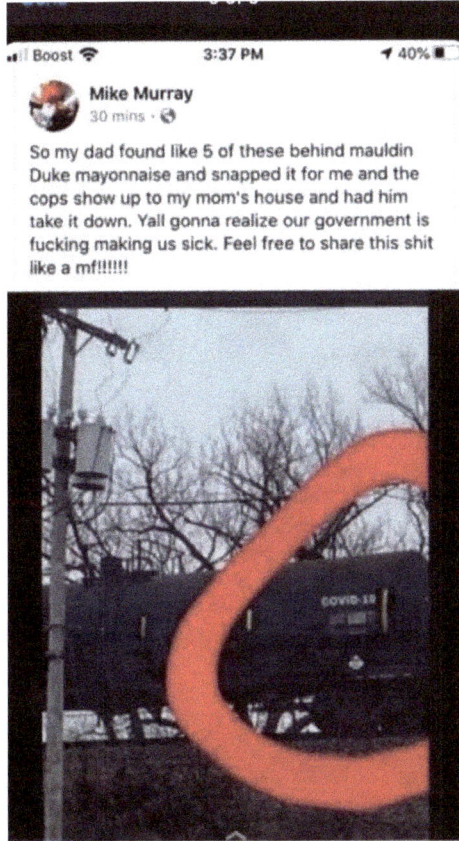

Source: [3]

I will let you decide.

[3] https://www.facebook.com/photo.php?fbid=2537571976 568973&set=a.1400298436963005&type=3&theater accessed March 30th 2020

CHAPTER 1

WHAT IS CORONAVIRUS?

Before we explain coronavirus, let us discuss what a virus is. First of all, a virus is not a living organism. It tends to come alive once it finds its way into a living host.

Dr Bruce Lipton expertly put it in this way:

'A virus is like a memory Stem. By itself, it is useless unless when plugged into a computer.'

The information stored in a memory card becomes useful and accessible only when it is being read through the screen of a computer device. The virus is similar to the memory card in that by itself outside a living host, it cannot function.

A virus is a capsule with a membrane-like envelope that contains information to control the genetics of a host-cell. Inside their host, they possess certain features needed for them to thrive and pass on their information to the host. And the information they contain compromises a rather functioning system.

The information on that virus memory is transferred to the cell which then takes over the cell, taking over its character as well as the metabolism of the cell. Viruses end up replicating themselves, establishing themselves by gradually killing the cells of the host which in turn ends up killing the host! Bad news!

According to the official narrative, coronavirus (COVID-19) is as follows:

Overview

According to the World Health Organization, Coronavirus (COVID-19) is an infectious disease caused by a newly discovered coronavirus. The COVID-19 virus spreads primarily through droplets of saliva or discharge from the nose when an infected person coughs or sneezes.

Symptoms

The symptoms of coronavirus are:

- Fever over 100.4 F (38 C)
- Aching muscles
- Shortness of breath

- Headache
- Dry, persistent cough
- Fatigue and weakness
- Nasal congestion
- Sore throat

But these symptoms do not necessarily mean that you have the illness. The symptoms are similar to other illnesses that are much more common, such as the common cold and flu.

Prevention

Do:

- wash your hands with soap and water often – do this for at least 20 seconds
- always wash your hands when you get home or into work
- use hand sanitiser gel if soap and water are not available
- cover your mouth and nose with a tissue or your sleeve (not your hands) when you cough or sneeze
- put used tissues in the bin straight away and wash your hands afterwards
- try to avoid close contact with people

Don't

- touch your eyes, nose or mouth if your hands are not clean

Treatments

There's no specific treatment for coronavirus (COVID-19). Treatment aims to relieve the symptoms until you recover.

You'll need to stay in isolation away from other people until you've recovered.[4]

I see that most experts and government agents tend to believe and run with the official narrative. Along with the 'SHEEPLE' too. I beg to differ but most people I know THINK that I am CRAZY! The 'eggspurts,' agents and SHEEPLE say that WE are now faced with UNCERTAIN times; the COVID-19 global pandemic, worldwide governmental lockdown and the looming global collapse of our economies, businesses, and financial markets.

But can we really TRUST the views and opinions of these folk? Can WE TRUST the NEWS from MAINSTREAM MEDIA? Can WE TRUST that OUR governments have our best interests at hearts? Is it possible that there is a power play here and some people are working towards their own gains and agendas? Can WE TRUST the SHEEPLE to give US TRUTH or SHOW us the right direction? I would want you to think about this.

8

---

4   https://www.who.int/health-topics/coronavirus accessed March 20th 2020 @15:55

Some people think I am crazy. But I know how I THINK and FEEL. I am screaming at the top of my voice that something sinister is going on but no one wants to listen. I am going to say my truth anyway.

Please take a look at the following:

1) **Videophones, Facetime, etc**. were predicted in The Simpsons cartoon show in 1995 but never came out in real life until 2010.5
2) **Smartwatches** were also predicted in The Simpsons in 1994 but never came out until 2014.6

---

5   Season 6 Episode 19

3) **Go Pro** the camera that we use to take photos came out in the Simpsons in 1994 but didn't come out until 2004 in real life.7

4) **Faulty voting machines** were shown in The Simpsons in 1994 when Homer tries to vote for Obama but there was a fault on the voting machine which meant that his vote went to John Mcain.

The strangest thing is that a similar thing happened in real life back in 2012 when it was highlighted and widely recognized the fact that someone had voted for Barack Obama and their vote went to Mitt Romney as the machine was deemed to have not been calibrated properly.8

5) In 2000, The Simpsons predicted that Donald Trump would be the president of the United States. This actually happened in 2016 and he is still the president now.9

I can go on and on about this sort of stuff and I will. YOU need to KNOW WHAT IS HAPPENING! It is only fair and right. And in future, you can give your children accurate information. What you do with this KNOWLEDGE is entirely up to YOU. Let US proceed.

---

6   Season 6 Episode 19

7   Season 5 Episode 13

8   Season 20 Episode 4

9   Season 11 Episode 17

6) In 2007, The Simpsons highlighted issues with the NSA (National Security Agency) spying on people. This came to pass in real life in 2013 when famous whistle-blower Edward Snowdon broke his silence to the world exposing the NSA and their extreme and highly unethical mass surveillance on us.[10]

7) In 2010, The Simpsons predicted the 2016 Nobel Prize winner.[11]

8) In 1998, they highlighted the corruption within FIFA which only became common KNOWLEDGE to US in 2012.[12]

Imagine that?

9) In 1998, they broke down The Higgs Boson which shows how the God particle relates to mathematics and the universe, this theory did not come out until 2012, how strange?[13]

10) In 1997, there was an outbreak of Ebola in the U.S. But in real life, this didn't happen until 2014.[14]

How is this?

11

---

10 The Simpsons Movie

11 Season 22 Episode 1

12 Season 25 Episode 16

13 Season 10 Episode 2

14 Season 9 Episode 3

11) In 2012, The Simpsons predicted the collapse of Greece's financial systems which actually occurred in 2015 as many of us are AWARE.[15]
12) In 1993, they predicted Ray Horn's tiger attack which happened in 2003.[16]

How uncanny?

13) In 2012, The Simpsons showed Lady Gaga's Superbowl halftime show which also happened in 2017 at Super bowl 51 in almost an identical manner.[17]
14) In 1998, it showed Disney as the owner of Fox, a 52 billion dollar deal, which didn't occur until nearly 20 years later (2017).
15) Then there is the BIG ONE!
16) Prince sang a song about this one a long time before the actual event. The Simpsons predicted it in 1997.[18] The **9/11 FAKE TERROR ATTACKS**. It is COMMON KNOWLEDGE THAT THERE WAS SOME TRICKERY AT PLAY HERE. WE, THE PUBLIC, WERE LIED TO ALSO. Facts were distorted by the media.

Right now, all I can do is SPEAK and show YOU that WE ARE OFTEN DECEIVED BY THE ONES WHO

---

15 Season 23 Episode 10

16 Season 5 Episode 10

17 Season 23 Episode 22

18 Season 9 Episode 1

SHOULD BE CARING FOR US. THE ONES WE NOMINATE. THE ONES WE ENTRUST WITH OUR LIVES. THE ONES IN GOVERNMENT. YES!

Far too many times The Simpson have predicted future events, a very strange phenomenon but also very true as you can see. I have left a link below for your perusal, there are many more examples there.

https://www.cheatsheet.com/entertainment/times-the-simpsons-predicted-the-future.html/19

It is a very sick way of entertainment for all parties if you ask me. It's a sick game. Just many do not see it. WHAT DO WE EXPERIENCE TOMORROW? Another EBOLA? Something related to SWINE FLU? Or another pandemic like COVID-19? It makes YOU wonder who the greatest prophet is: Is it The Mayans? The Egyptians? Nostradamus? Edgar Cayce? Elijah Muhammad? Dr Malachi Z. York? Or is it HOMER SIMPSON?

At this rate, Homer Simpson would win it hands down.

The Simpsons isn't the only show that deals with predictions, Star Trek used to do it, Futurama does it also as well as many other shows, movies and books. Have you watched the movie Contagion which was released in 2011?

Check out the trailer below:

https://youtu.be/4sYSyuuLk5g20

13

---

19 Accessed March 21st @18:37

They appear to be talking about the current outbreak of coronavirus many, many years ago but the same thing that happened in the movie is the same thing that is happening now.

Check out the next series, which is on Netflix, this one even mentions a coronavirus outbreak:

Isn't that not serious enough to be used as a weapon?

the mortality rate was over 20 percent.

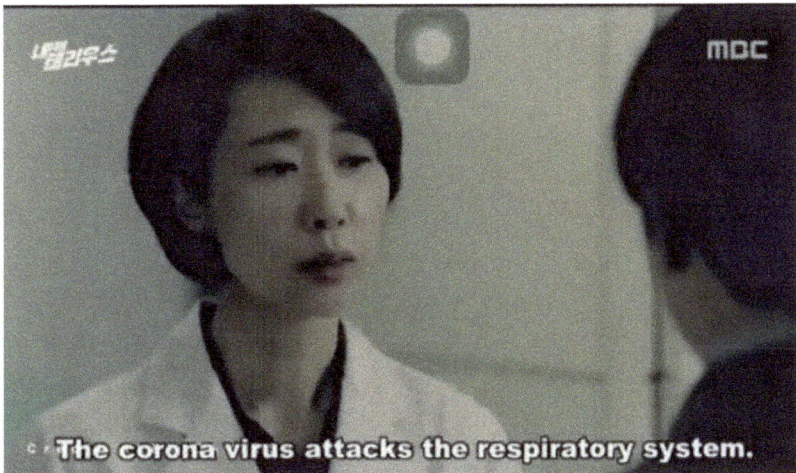

The corona virus attacks the respiratory system.

15

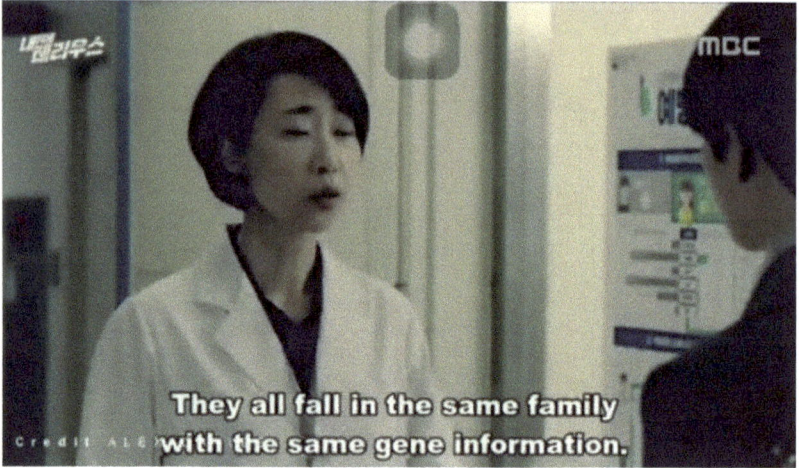

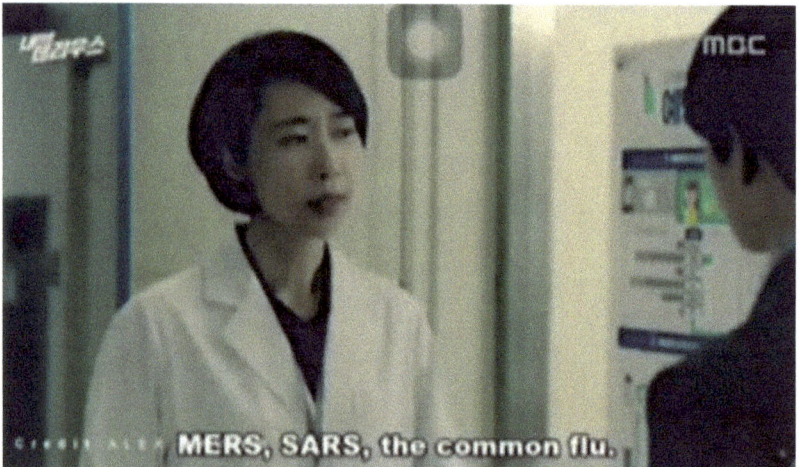

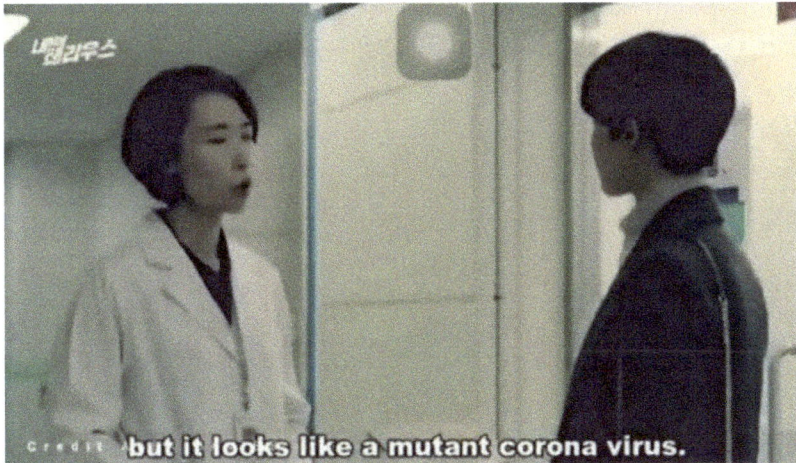

My Secret Terrius came out in 2018. How did they know about this?

The funny thing is, Bill Gates described this whole phenomenon (exactly how is) at a televised conference in 2015 saying, what if this outbreak of contagious disease was to hit the world and spread rapidly.

Please check out the link below and you can see for yourself:

https://africacheck.org/fbcheck/bill-gates-did-warn-in-2015-of-possible-global-virus-outbreak-but-not-coronavirus-specifically/21

He described the outcome to a tee albeit four years before the actual event. Predictive programming is the

---

21 Accessed March 21st @18:52

ORDER of the DAY I FEEL. You may see I am just being PARANOID. But AM I?

Also, kindly check out the next link where this current coronavirus has allegedly been predicted on The Simpson, but that one is up for debate:

https://youtu.be/rv-U-idfLbQ 22

https://www.youtube.com/watch?v=v53GmsuppwY&feature=youtu.be 23

Do you realize what is coming next? From what WE can SEE here it is quite obvious that some entities have been trying to CREATE OUR FUTURES with varying degrees of SUCCESS.

First, they PLAN OUR FUTURE. Then they PREDICT IT (that is where the predictive programming comes in). Then they CREATE it. THEY HAVE THE MONEY, POWER, RESOURCES and WE ARE LEFT WITH THE PAPER. However, ALL is not LOST. WE JUST NEED TO STOP GIVING AWAY OUR POWERS. STOP GIVING AWAY OUR MINDS! AND STOP GIVING AWAY OUR SOULS!

WE NEED TO SHOW DIVINE LOVE TO EACH OTHER, SERVING EACH OTHER WHEN AND WHERE NECESSARY. WE NEED TO STOP BEING SUBMISSIVE

19

---

22 Accessed March 21st @18:55

23 Accessed March 21st @18:55

MIND-CONTROLLED SLAVE SHEEP – IT IS NOT COOL.
Many people RELY ON OUR GOVERNMENTS TOO
MUCH. YES, people need them. Many OF us cannot
cope without them WHICH IS VERY SAD IF YOU ASK
ME. But we should not LET OURSELVES BE IN THIS
position as WE ARE now.

WE should take control of our own affairs, of our own
lives, CREATE OUR OWN MAGIC, and OUR OWN
FUTURES. Why should WE let anyone treat US this
WAY? I KNOW it is not an easy TIME OUT there at the
moment, I realize that there is so much going on. So
much panic and so much fear, believe it or not, it is all
part of a PLAN just one that WE didn't CREATE.

If you have read to this point, then don't despair, we
have SOLUTIONS. And all is not LOST. IT IS OUR TIME
NOW. AND THEY KNOW THIS. But if you are yet to get
the point, I'll keep explaining.

Take a look at the picture below:

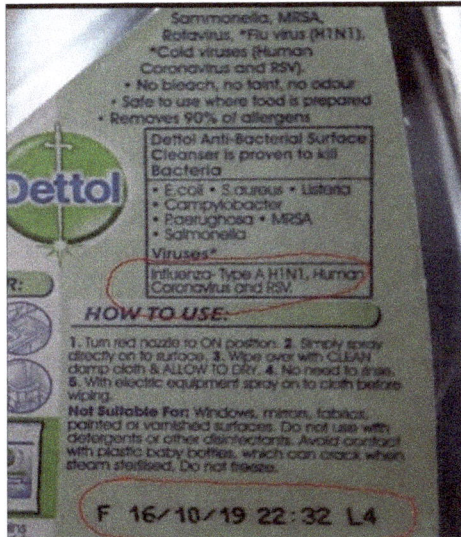

Don't you find it strange that coronavirus is on the back of Dettol containers? Perhaps, there is nothing to it and my thoughts are going wild. But take a LOOK at this... I did a quick search on duckduckgo.com and guess what came up:

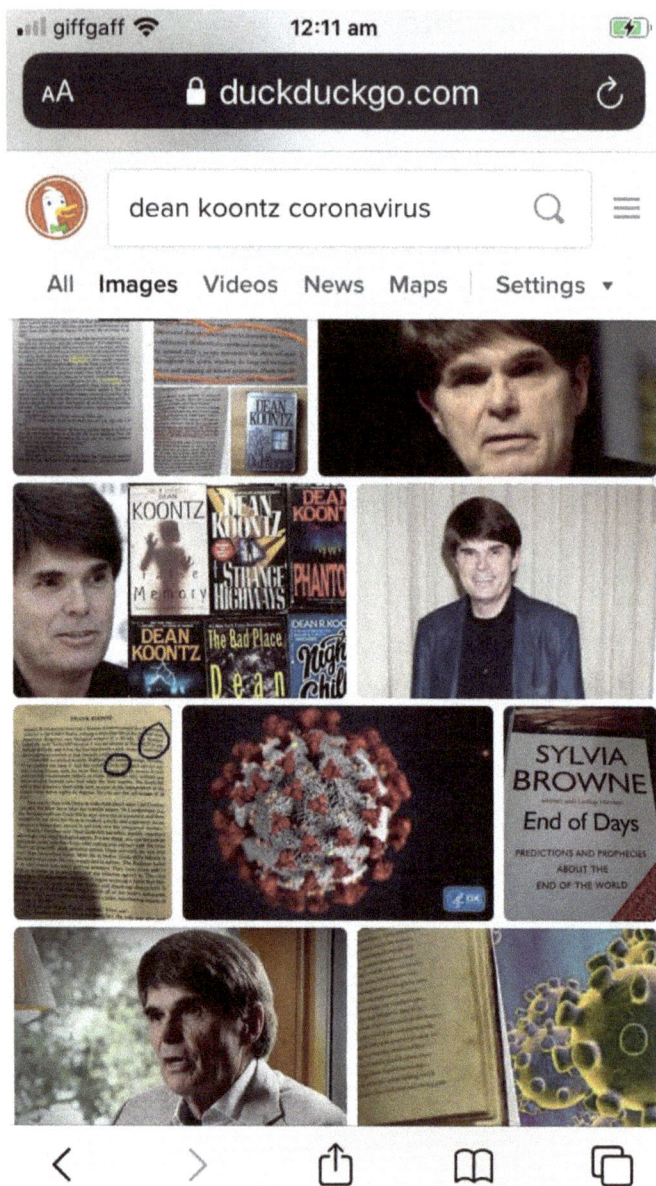

23

Strange! Isn't it

What is going on?

I would love to just finish off this chapter with a quote:

"A courageous person is not a fool; they are a successful man or woman who does what THEY WANT to ACHIEVE THEIR GOALS.

REMEMBER, people who have no GOALS, have NO WAY, NO PURPOSE.

If we teach our CHILDREN to CONFORM to a FAILING SYSTEM or SOCIETY, then WE have FAILED already.

WE ARE THE POWER."

– Dr Kwadw(o) Naya: Baa Ankh Em Ra A'lyun Eil

CHAPTER 2

QUESTIONS

Let us start with a few questions:

Sometimes anomalies are sprung on us which appear to have more questions than answers. Coronavirus is a perfect example of this.

1) Is COVID-19 manmade? And if it is, are the conspiracy theories real? And if not, what was the cause and how do we react to this?
2) What are the effects of COVID-19 on the nations of the world? What are the medical, economical and lifestyle implications? It's been said that COVID-19 will change the world forever. But in what way exactly?
3) What is the position of the World Health Organization? Are they complicit in this? Did they do enough to reduce the scourge of this virus?

Why has Donald Trump cut their budget for next year? What about the CDC? What are they doing to make sure this public health disorder doesn't happen again? Why did President Trump fall out with them?

4) What was the role of China in all these? Is it true that coronavirus originated from Wuhan?

5) What has Dr.Fauchi, the director of the National Institute of Allergy and Infectious Diseases (NIAID), got to do with all this? Why is his name even mentioned at all?

6) Why are the testing kits faulty? What are the pros and cons of the different testing kits?

7) Vaccines. Vaccines. Vaccines. Are they necessary? The authorities are bringing out different vaccines as I write this. I thought vaccines take 3-5 years to be produced? How come they have been produced in such a short time?

8) What are doctors all over the world saying about this? There are a lot of differing opinions about the best way to manage this virus.

9) How can we protect ourselves and families from COVID-19 and any other future pandemic?

CHAPTER 3

STATISTICS

As I write this, things are looking bad. So many people, both young and old, have died in such a short time.

Let US have a LOOK at the official figures.

As of 07:39 am on May 10th 2020, 4,155,268 cases of COVID-19 have been confirmed, with 1,467,062 people who have recovered and 282,771 total deaths.[24] These numbers are worrisome. So much death in just a couple of months. This is why the nations of the world are panicking. It's causing FEAR and nations are coming up with UNCONVENIET AND TOUGH COUNTERMEASURES.

---

[24] https://gisanddata.maps.arcgis.com/apps/opsdashboard/index.html#/bda7594740fd40299423467b48e9ecf6 accessed March 26th 2020 @06:21

I am sure the world will not remain after this pandemic. It's funny, WE never really hear about the stories of people who have recovered. The media only share the number of people that have died. But they make less noise about those that have recovered. Well, as humans we do relate more to negative emotions than positive ones. But the stories of those recovering would warm hearts and inspire hope.

There has been no clarity in testing procedures. The tests have been inaccurate on several occasions where people have received positive results when they were perfectly well. How many times has this happened? Will we never know?

There are many coronaviruses, all of which, appear to have been created in laboratories. Please check out this patent below, it is a patent for a previous strain of coronavirus:

https://patents.google.com/patent/US7220852B1/en

There was also a patent for the current coronavirus but there seems to be some controversy behind it if YOU TAKE A LOOK YOU WILL SEE! Why are they making viruses anyway? Is there any need?

Did you know that the biggest virus making institute is in WUHAN?

According to Wikipedia, The Wuhan Institute of Virology, Chinese Academy of Sciences is a research institute on virology administered by the Chinese

Academy of Sciences. Located in Jiangxia District, Wuhan, Hubei, it opened mainland China's first biosafety level 4 laboratory in 2015.

WE ALL KNOW what happens when these viruses are released. We have all seen it time and time again. COVID-19 is supposedly sponsored by Bill Gates AND The Clinton Foundation Dr Shiva has most recently confirmed this. Check his video out below. It is a must watch as he reveals real truths about viruses, government corruption and cover-ups. He also goes through COVID-19 detailing the current situation. It is a must-watch.

I have left the full version for your perusal:[25]

https://www.youtube.com/watch?v=xf-qv9o8nq8

Please make sure that you watch this video. Last time I checked, it had over five million views. It will open your eyes to a thing or two.

With the current coronavirus, it looks like they have done a very good job. Whilst it is not as bad as some illnesses, it works in a way that attacks the immune and respiratory system, which can have devastating effects.

Old people, people with existing health issues, and young people who have bad diets and live unhealthily

---

25 https://www.youtube.com/watch?v=1BiM1YYIPCo accessed April 11th 2020 @23:51

tend to have a weakened immune system. These are the people that are more liable to struggle with the new COVID-19.

Now, why will anyone want to make viruses? Does that even make sense? Does it have any health care significance? Is our healthcare system going backwards on PURPOSE? The treatment being used at the moment doesn't CURE PEOPLE but that is another STORY. Medication does help treat the symptoms but not the cause. We are addressing and CURING the SYMPTOMS but NOT the REAL PROBLEM.

It is LIKE a BUSINESS. A LARGE GLOBAL CONGLOMERATE. They are in the BUSINESS of BEING in BUSINESS. Not in the BUSINESS of HELPING PEOPLE. We ALL KNOW that coronavirus is promoted BIG in the media. You have seen it all over the news. The symptoms, the deaths, the FEAR, ANXIETY, PANIC. They hardly promote the GOOD SIDE, just the DOOM and GLOOM which makes one SUSPICIOUS.

The coronavirus symptoms, as spoke about in chapter one, are similar to many viruses and cases of the flu. It LOOKS to me that whenever anyone is showing any traits of these symptoms it is DEEMED that they have coronavirus.

Another thing that happened and is still happening is that this won't be the first time we have experienced this. This won't be the first time a highly contagious virus is in circulation and killing people all over the world. But OUR MEDICAL industry always feigns ignorance and do not have a CURE for the illness.

Why are large players across the globe suddenly rushing to produce a vaccine? How safe will these vaccines be? How can WE be expected to go or even put OUR TRUST in the hands of medical professionals who don't even have the tools, knowledge, know-how or competency to carry out what they are doing? How are we supposed to deal with this with over two hundred thousand deaths and millions hurting?

More than four million people have shown symptoms of coronavirus. How do we know that they were affected by COVID-19 considering all the factors I just mentioned? How can OUR medical INDUSTRY HEAL these people when they have an incorrect approach to treating illnesses? They do not have sufficient, correct, or even any resources to deal with illnesses under their current prognosis(s)?

CYCLING IS BAD FOR THE ECONOMY

Hilarious but true too

A cyclist is a disaster for the country's economy -
He does not buy the car & does not take a car loan -
Does not buy car insurance - Does not buy Fuel -
Does not send his car for servicing & repairs -
Does not use paid Parking - Does not become Obese

Yes,.....and well, damn it !! Healthy people are not needed
for economy. They do not buy drugs. They do not go to
Hospitals & Doctors. They add nothing to country's GDP.
On the contrary, every new fast food outlet creates at least
30 jobs - 10 Cardiologists, 10 Dentists, 10 weight loss
experts apart from people working in the outlet. Choose
wisely: A Cyclist or a KFC ? Worth thinking about!!

PS: Walking is even worse. They do not even buy a bicycle!!

Credit: Picture from Pramod Simon Facebook Post

"I bike EVERYWHERE!! I would love a car, but not when it costs an arm and a leg just to keep it running! I'd rather stay fit and enjoy the fresh air!"

A statement made by someone on his Facebook post. You can see how people think all this is a joke. You can read the comments about the post here:

https://web.facebook.com/photo.php?fbid=327853983
9037115&set=a.18391358063108 66&type=3&theater&_
rdc=1&_rdr

A few weeks ago, I displayed COVID-19 symptoms. I contacted my GP (General Practitioner) and was advised to contact 111 which I did. They advised me to quarantine myself for two weeks and said I would receive a letter in 3 working days with further instructions, which would also tell me when they were coming to test me. Fortunately for me, no letter come. I was not tested either. They say one thing and do another - quite impressive! But if we did it back to them it is a problem? What a nice world WE live in! For the record, I do not generally seek advice from a GP as I prefer natural remedies. They tend to work better in my experience.

At the moment, schools are closed. Parents are worried. Here is a short transcript from a contact on my WhatsApp:

"I can't wait to play with my friends!"

"Well yeah, you might see some of your friends, but you won't be able to touch them or play with them."

"Why?"

"Because of the germs."

"But there aren't any now?"

"Right... but might be...so you can't go close to your friends."

"Oh well, at least I'll see them."

"Well, you might not see them all because you might not all be in the same classroom."

"Oh, but I'll be in my classroom though right?"

"Well, you might not be because you'll have to spread out a bit."

"Spread out to where?"

"To other classrooms."

"But won't the other classes be in their rooms?"

"No the other classes won't be there."

"Why?"

"Because of the germs."

"But why am I the only one going back?"

"Umm...because you're small and you can spread out more?...because you don't take up so much space?! Honestly, no one knows mate."

"Oh well, at least I'll see my teacher...but wait ...Mum, how will my teacher be in the classrooms at once?"

"Well, you might not have your teacher."

"Who will I have?"

"I don't know..."

"Oh... if I'm going back to school can we go and get my new school shoes? Remember you said I would have to get new shoes because my feet have grown?!"

"Right...yeah...it's not safe to open the shops so we can't get shoes."

"But it is safe for me to go to school?"

"Yes, maybe...unless there's a spike in the virus, then we might have to stay home again."

"How will they know if there's a spike in the virus though mum? Hospitals admissions... and the number of deaths."

"But what if I've already got it by then, from going to school?"

"Well, you probably won't die because you're young."

"Do children not die then?"

"Most of them don't but grownups do? Some, yes."

"So what about my teacher? Mum is it ok if I don't go back to school? It doesn't sound like it's the right time yet?"

"Yes mate that's fine, you're right, let's stay home."

I guess they were reacting to the news that the UK government wants children to still go to school: https://www.itv.com/thismorning/hot-topics/matt-hancock-offers-clarity-on-government-guidelines

So if she is this disturbed and confused you can imagine what is going on in the minds of millions all over the world.

Here are a few more voices of concerned and worried people: https://www.theguardian.com/world/2020/feb/26/coronavirus-uk-will-paid-take-sick-leave

So let me guess what you believe:

1) COVID-19 doesn't exist it's a Hoax
2) COVID-19 is 5G
3) China released COVID-19
4) COVID-19 emerged from people in China eating BATS
5) EBOLA emerged from Africans somehow mingling with Monkeys?

All you guys need to do is google EBOLA, research the way the press created euphoria, sensationalization, condemnation, negative stereotypes and its condescending narrative.

A few factual points about the EBOLA narrative:

1) EBOLA came from monkeys
2) Ebola thrives due to a dirty environment and lack of personal hygiene
3) Africans were afraid of WHO personnel because they were seen to be the ones transferring and infecting others with Ebola.
4) vaccine
5) Second wave concerns.

37

We then find out that EBOLA is a laboratory-made virus just like COVID-19. These points show a classic behavioral pattern of biowarfare and media propaganda which has also been implemented concerning COVID-19. But this time around, the

WESTERN NATIONS have been affected by the BIOWARFARE

A LEOPARD DOESN'T CHANGE ITS SPOTS!

I understand for Western Carbonites (misnomer: [blacks]), it would look confusing but for Africans who have always been suspicious about colonisers and the Chinese, Africans who observe everything with scrutiny, would have straight away seen this as the biowarfare playbook 101 narratives.

Ebola was created in the Bill and Melinda Gates Foundation - you will find.

COVID-19 is biowarfare against china by the USA that has got out of hand. The virus transferred from the USA to a china laboratory. The virus was released during trade talks.

But now something more advanced has been planned. Between 2020 and 2030, there is a global plan to decimate and imprison humanity and alter lifestyles choices that will suit their evil agenda. This is not a conspiracy. There are verifiable facts.

You can check it out here:

https://web.facebook.com/watch/?v=153334561019159
2

It's a grand design plan by the United Nations and its called Agenda 2030.

Since early February, I have constantly driven home the point that the science bringing the world this COVID-19 pandemic is rife with bad practices. WITHOUT a highly-functioning, highly-specific and DIRECT test for this pathogen, there is no way to know just who is or is not infected. Without a test, you do not have an epidemic of an infectious disease. Do YOU want to get tested using these highly flawed antibody assays? After all, this Abbott Laboratory test is used at the White House; that's good enough for you, right?

Take a few minutes to read the following and perhaps SAVE YOUR LIFE!

Accuracy of rapid coronavirus test called into question by NYU study, by DAVID LIM.

https://www.politico.com/news/2020/05/13/rapid-coronavirus-test-accuracy-nyu-study-256351

Conclusion

Overall, our study revealed low sensitivity with high false-negative results by Abbott ID NOW platform irrespective of the use of viral transport media, which raises concern regarding the performance of the assay and its suitability as a diagnostic tool for symptomatic patients. The resolution could be to reflex all negative results for confirmation by a method with higher sensitivity. However, such a requirement would, except for positives, severely diminish the value of the rapid results of the assay.

Performance of the rapid Nucleic Acid Amplification by Abbott ID NOW COVID-19 in nasopharyngeal swabs transported in viral media and dry nasal swabs, in a New York City academic institution, by Atreyee Basu, Tatyana Zinger, Kenneth Inglima, Kar-mun Woo, Onomie Atie, Lauren Yurasits, Benjamin See, and Maria E. Aguero-Rosenfeld, NYU Grossman School of Medicine, Department of Pathology, NYU Langone Health, Tisch Hospital, NYU Grossman School of Medicine, Department of Emergency Medicine, New York – https://www.biorxiv.org/content/10.1101/2020.05.11.089896v1.full.pdf

Some of you will not accept that I am capable of dissecting this scientific literature on the failure of antibody assays as reliable diagnostic technology. No problem. Read it for yourself and then report to me your conclusions.

67. CDC Tests for COVID-19 - https://www.cdc.gov/coronavirus/2019-ncov/about/testing.html

68. Coronavirus and the race to distribute reliable diagnostics - https://www.nature.com/articles/d41587-020-00002-2

69. What you need to know about coronavirus testing in the U.S. - https://www.sciencenews.org/.../coronavirus-testing...

70. Correlation of Chest CT and RT-PCR Testing in Coronavirus Disease 2019 (COVID-19) in China: A Report of 1014 Cases - https://pubs.rsna.org/doi/10.1148/radiol.2020200642

71. Comparing RT-PCR and Chest CT for Diagnosing COVID-19, by Adam Sturt, MARCH 17, 2020 - https://www.mdmag.com/.../comparing-rt-pcr-and-chest-ct...

72. Blood Test: Immunoglobulins (IgA, IgG, IgM) - https://kidshealth.org/en/parents/test-immunoglobulins.html

73. COVID-19 IgG/IgM Rapid Test Kit (Whole Blood/Serum/Plasma) For Professional Use

74. Potential False-Positive Rate Among the 'Asymptomatic Infected Individuals' in Close Contacts of COVID-19 Patients, Zhonghua Liu Xing Bing Xue Za Zhi, 41 (4), 485-488 2020 Mar 5 - https://pubmed.ncbi.nlm.nih.gov/32133832

75. FDA publishes first validation results of 12 COVID-19 antibody tests, by Conor Hale, May 8, 2020 - https://www.fiercebiotech.com/.../fda-publishes-first...

76. THE DISAPPOINTING TRUTH ABOUT ANTIBODY TESTING, By Elizabeth Lopatto@mslopatto May 7, 2020 - https://www.theverge.com/.../coronavirus-antibody-tests...

101. How FDA Plans to Tackle Coronavirus Serology Tests ... For Now, Apr 16, 2020 | Madeleine Johnson - https://www.360dx.com/immunoassays/how-fda-plans-tackle-coronavirus-serology-tests-now#.XpnHSMhKjIU

102. An Antibody Test for COVID-19 Has Been Developed in New York, by Serena McNiff 08 April - https://live.healthday.com/covid-antibody-tests-developed-for-use-in-new-york-state-2645669458.html

103. Study Raises Questions About False Negatives From Quick COVID-19 Test, April 21, 20206:07, by Rob

Stein - https://www.npr.org/sections/health-shots/2020/04/21/838794281/study-raises-questions-about-false-negatives-from-quick-covid-19-test

104. DETECT COVID-19 IN AS LITTLE AS 5 MINUTES - https://www.abbott.com/corpnewsroom/product-and-innovation/detect-covid-19-in-as-little-as-5-minutes.html

105. ID NOW™ COVID-19 MOLECULAR. - https://www.alere.com/en/home/product-details/id-now-covid-19.html

106. ID NOW™ COVID-19 MOLECULAR. IN MINUTES™, ON THE FRONT LINE - https://ensur.invmed.com/ensur/contentAction.aspx?key=ensur.516354.S2R4E4A3.20200328.10292.4355032

107. Abbott ID NOW™ COVID-19 PRODUCT INSERT - https://ensur.invmed.com/ensur/contentAction.aspx?key=ensur.514295.S2R4E4A3.20200328.10292.4358420

108. EXPERTS: US WILL NEED 20 MILLION TESTS PER DAY TO REOPEN SAFELY, BY VICTOR TANGERMANN / APRIL 20, 2020 - https://futurism.com/neoscope/experts-20-million-tests-per-day

109. Coronavirus Testing Needs to Triple Before the U.S. Can Reopen, Experts Say, By Keith Collins, April 17, 2020 - https://www.nytimes.com/interactive/2020/04/17/us/coronavirus-testing-states.html

When was the cares and coronavirus economic act written? You will think it was after the coronavirus started. But you will find out otherwise:

https://www.instagram.com/p/B_0KE0JpBN3/?fbclid= IwAR0RQ791lP8mR3- q9rlG6Ii2IwelFA0yB7lB5jyYIPtxIrdahwHmi9rABVg

Check out the following statement from Alex Aquarius:

> "*I agree with David as a vaccine manufacturing, marketing and sales expert. I was taught about TR-PCR tests A.K.A. Genetic Fingerprinting when I sold vaccines for a division of Eli Lilly Elanco in Latin America and Europe. Humans have already had 6 known coronaviruses. I was looking at them under a microscope and taught by Pathologist friends at work. You do have to isolate the virus to know the code, and the tests are hard to come by. This 5-minute test Trump talked about. Is it a visual analog corona test when we have already 6 past coronaviruses? Visually, it looks like a crown under the microscope in 2D on a slide. X-rays are looking for pneumonia plaques ind alveolar clusters. That could be anything even the influenza.*"[26]

---

26 https://www.youtube.com/watch?v=Yg-GC8AW6cc accessed April 28th 2020 @00:24

We need to stay focused and positive and take care of ourselves. The next chapter is all about SOLUTIONS. I will SEE YOU there!

CHAPTER 4

SOLUTIONS

I live in the United Kingdom. I do not KNOW what the united about it. We were put on house arrest by Boris Johnson OUR prime minister. The ONE that WE nominated to run things and take care of OUR behalf.

This happened on March 23rd 2020. Boris Johnson told us to stay at home. He advised us that we were only to come out of OUR homes for the following reasons:

1) Shopping for basic necessities (food or medicine [once a day])
2) One form of exercise a day – for example, a walk, run or maybe a ride on your bike alone or with another member of your household
3) Any medical appointments or emergencies or to provide care to help a vulnerable person

4) Travelling to and from work, but only where absolutely necessary.

He also brought in the policy of social distancing.

I think that it is TIME that WE started taking control of OUR AFFAIRS. What would you say? As these people who WE nominate and TRUST always seem to end UP KILLING, HURTING and FORCING US to be ENSLAVED.

Besides, prime ministers, presidents, and government officials have a habit of breaking their own rules whilst expecting us to adhere. We only have to look at Boris Johnson's chief adviser, Dominic Cummings, who broke lockdown 'stay at home' rules by traveling to Barnard Castle (a 52-mile round trip). Boris Johnson stated that he believed Mr Cummings behaved reasonably and legally and regards the issue as closed. Why is it one rule for one, and one rule for another?

The WORST thing is the FACT that the WORLD is FULL of SELL OUTS and SHEEPLE. Unfortunately, most of US can be ILLUDED, TRICKED, BOUGHT AND SOLD. Are LAW ENFORCEMENT AGENCIES a CLASSIC EXAMPLE? Whatever happened to HUMANITY? WHATEVER HAPPENED TO LOOKING AFTER GAIA (MOTHER EARTH)? I guess that never fits into to the world of GLOBAL BUSINESS.

I read this interesting article:

> **"UK downgrades COVID-19; no longer a high consequence infectious disease**
>
> *Where is the media roar all over the world---blasting out the news that the UK government no longer considers COVID an existential threat to all life on Earth? No giant headlines indicating that the dominos are now starting to fall in another direction---away from sheer suicidal insanity. Oh, that's right, it's the MEDIA.*
>
> *The UK government, on its website, announced on March 23, under "Status of COVID-19": "As of 19 March 2020, COVID-19 is no longer considered to be a high consequence infectious diseases (HCID) in the UK. BANG."* 27

You can find the official notifications of this on the gov.uk website but I will leave it below for your pursual.

> **High consequence infectious diseases (HCID)**
>
> *Guidance and information about high consequence infectious diseases and their management in England.*
>
> **Status of COVID-19**

---

27 Email from Jon Rappoport info@nomorefakenews.com received @March 26th 2020 @00:43

As of 19 March 2020, COVID-19 is no longer considered to be a high consequence infectious diseases (HCID) in the UK.

The 4 nations public health HCID group made an interim recommendation in January 2020 to classify COVID-19 as an HCID. This was based on consideration of the UK HCID criteria about the virus and the disease with information available during the early stages of the outbreak. Now that more is known about COVID-19, the public health bodies in the UK have reviewed the most up to date information about COVID-19 against the UK HCID criteria. They have determined that several features have now changed; in particular, more information is available about mortality rates (low overall), and there is now greater clinical awareness and a specific and sensitive laboratory test, the availability of which continues to increase.

The Advisory Committee on Dangerous Pathogens (ACDP) is also of the opinion that COVID-19 should no longer be classified as an HCID.

The need to have a national, coordinated response remains, but this is being met by the government's COVID-19 response.

Cases of COVID-19 are no longer managed by HCID treatment centres only. All healthcare workers managing possible and confirmed cases should

> *follow the <u>updated national infection and prevention (IPC) guidance for COVID-19</u>, which supersedes all previous IPC guidance for COVID-19. This guidance includes instructions about different personal protective equipment (PPE) ensembles that are appropriate for different clinical scenarios.28*

This is funny.

Why have WE been put on house arrest, with OUR LIBERTIES TAKEN AWAY FROM US, OUR LIVELIHOODS and BUSINESSES when as *of March 19 2020, COVID-19 was no longer deemed a high consequence infectious disease?* **This makes no sense UNLESS THESE PEOPLE HAVE ULTERIOR MOTIVES.**

It's TIME for them ALL to GO. Do you agree? Why do WE ALL put UP with this? THE TV says 'JUMP', WE SAY 'how HIGH?!' WE get put on house arrest under false pretences and MOST of US listen and FOLLOW like SUBMISSIVE SHEEP, buying into the PANIC, FEAR, STRESS and ANXIETY? What do you say to all of this?

Enough of this DOOM and GLOOM stuff. Let US get down to some solutions. Whenever I think of diseases my mind goes back to Dr Sebi a man renown for curing people of all illnesses many times over. He

51

---

28 https://www.gov.uk/guidance/high-consequence-infectious-diseases-hcid#status-of-covid-19 accessed 26th Mar 2020 @06:56

states that disease cannot live in an alkaline premise and advises that we should only be eating electric alkaline foods.

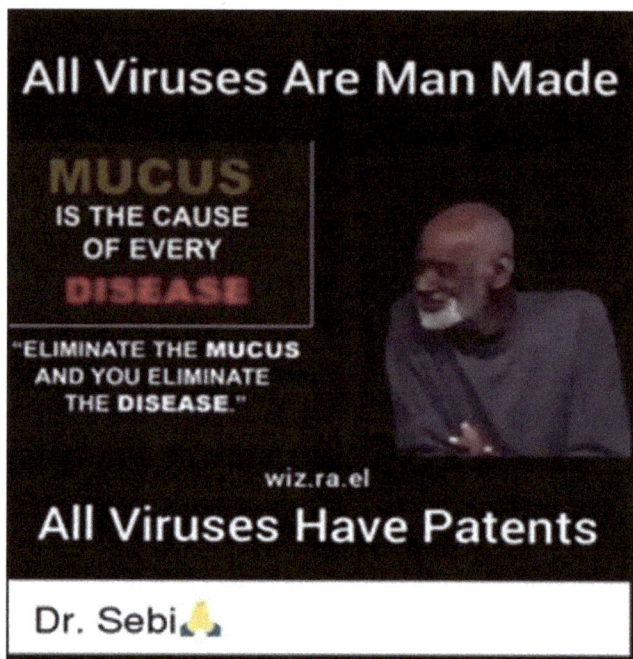

All Viruses Are Man Made

MUCUS IS THE CAUSE OF EVERY DISEASE

"ELIMINATE THE MUCUS AND YOU ELIMINATE THE DISEASE."

wiz.ra.el

All Viruses Have Patents

Dr. Sebi

If we did this, I am sure that no one would have died or been badly affected by the current coronavirus. YOU SEE, everybody is so scared but the main thing these man-made diseases target is the immune system. So that means boost your immune system by eating the right foods then your body will naturally kill off any bad pathogens. It is important to keep your body and health in prime condition, many of US take this for granted. But I realize that life is not perfect and that most of us do not have the best diet for our being or even the best health or fitness. But there is still plenty of solutions out there for US, I am not going to list them all, but I will list a good few, so if you ever get caught out you know what to do.

Many great HEALTH PROFESSIONALS in the FIELD have BIG WARM HEARTS and do a great job. It must be difficult for them sometimes given the tough conditions, the dodgy prognosis procedures (which they are contracted to adhere to, even if they know better) and limited resources that they are faced with. There are also some very BAD ones as we all know. Some do not THINK outside the box, they just follow instruction as they have been taught at medical school, and others are just simply no good at all.

Don't you THINK that it is a better option for US to be taking care of OUR own HEALTHCARE? Who cares about US more than US? Did YOU KNOW that the PHARMACEUTICAL industry is one of the BIGGEST if not the BIGGEST industry on the PLANET? Did YOU KNOW that PHARMACEUTICALS is BIG, BIG BUSINESS? Exactly! Can YOU SEE the contradictions? In US paying or even just taking UNNATURAL medicines which will often not CURE US but relieve the symptoms that we are experiencing?

53

I do not deal with the NHS (National Health Service) as I find natural remedies work best. Many of the pharmaceuticals are made from natural ingredients, with this in mind, wouldn't it be better to always go to the source? Deal with the NATURAL opposed to playing around or consuming the engineered SYNTHETICS.

I will start with the natural stuff first before moving onto some of the more conventional tests and procedures which one may prefer to go through. But before I start, I would just like to post an image, it seems quite fitting. I would appreciate your thoughts:

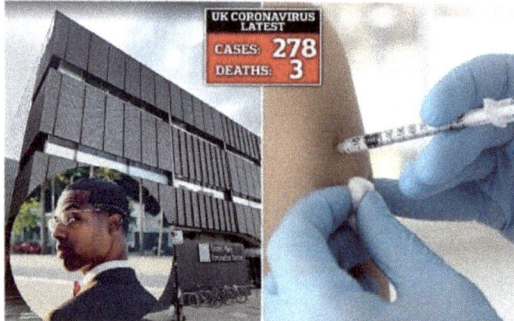

"But people are already being infected for FREE... But I guess not FAST ENOUGH right??? Probably comes with burial insurance just as they did during the Tuskegee experiment. Now tell me again how the #CoronvVirus ISN'T created by the government. They're PAYING YOU TO BE THE EXPERIMENT in order to speed up the process of creating a new "vaccine" (which normally takes 10 - 15 years to do). So people have the possibility of DYING for something that this government KNOWS can be cured with simple high

doses of VITAMIN C (Liposomal vitamin C) administered intravenously taken as tablets in high doses daily. They are NOT telling the public this of course because they will lose BILLIONS!!! The agenda is #depopulation! THINK 🐑🐑 *#rizzaislam #covid19 #rizzawithfacts #intellectualxtremist #WEAREFARRAKHAN.*29

It is bad for anyone to die I know, it should not happen like this, very sad and shocking indeed. But it is always good to look at the positives. Most people who get COVID-19 make a full recovery. Many, many people have opted to heal themselves with great results. Have you noticed that not many people are dying at home? Out of the over two hundred thousand people who died have you noticed that most of those people went to hospital, never to come out again?

55

---

29 https://www.facebook.com/rizzaislam1/photos/a.37 9990422142236/1715814548559810/?type=3&theater accessed April 4th 2020 @14:11

Some were given Ibuprofen or other similar drugs (which is no good for COVID-19) whilst others were given antivirals which had a similar effect. The question I ask is WHY is everyone is running to the National Health Service to save them when the very same people admit that they are working with a virus that they have no clue about? There is simply no cure. They don't know what they are doing. Nobody knows.

Let me share a video with you, I find it funny.

https://mobile.facebook.com/story.php?story_fbid=24 76736764740778&id=124411634236128%3Fsfnsn%3Dw a&d=w&vh=e&_rdc=1&_rdr

Can you believe what the Tanzania President did?

All I am saying is we should be very careful. We should not just focus on what is media is giving to us. We need to think deeply and observe what is happening.

Listen to a distressed nurse here:
https://www.youtube.com/watch?v=G4hJFCx6z_8&fea ture=youtu.be

She is in agony. Seeing a lot of people around her dying. No human should bear this. I bet even after reading this and going through the videos most of you all cannot wait to go and get the VACCINE. YOU will even give it to your CHILDREN. Is this not a CLASSIC CASE of COGNITIVE DISSONANCE?

Let us get back to the solutions, we will start with the natural and organic solutions first before moving onto the unnatural:

NATURAL REMEDIES

1) **Strong Immune system**
   If WE have a strong immune system WE cannot go WRONG.

   2) **Clean Strong Digestive tract** –

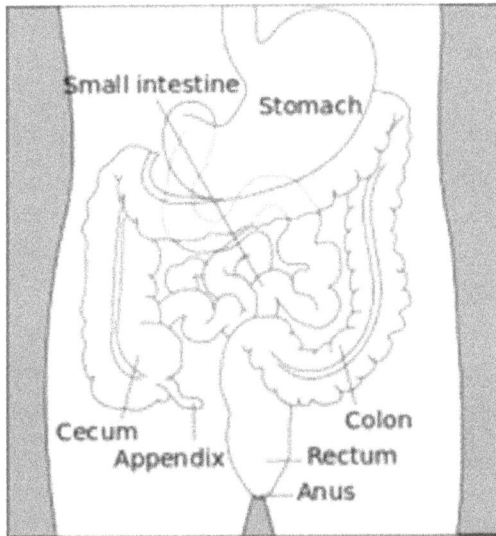

Our **digestive** systems are uniquely designed to turn the food that we consume into nutrients, which the body uses for energy, growth, and cell repair. Many of US never have this system cleaned out, which means that there will be years old rotting food in there, meat, bacteria, and germs, etc. which is bound to cause problems. Most of us have between 6 to 40 pounds of faecal matter stored between our colon and our small intestines and large intestines.

Can you IMAGINE?

The situation is easily resolved, WE just need to carry out a colon cleanse, check out Dr Sebi's website drsebicellfoods.com. You can find the stuff there if you get stuck. You could also go for colonic irrigation which would do just the trick. A cousin of mine has been for it twice and he says it works wonders.

3) Sea Moss and Bladderwrack

Our bodies are made up of 102 minerals which ideally, we should be taking through the food that we eat and drink for our bodies to be fully optimized.

Sea Moss and **Bladderwrack** contain 97 out of the 102 minerals (which is a great start), in which our body is made up of. Ideally, we need to consume these 102 minerals daily to be fully nourished. Sea Moss and Bladderwrack work in a way which seems to push the illness out of your body from the inside.

It is great stuff I have had it many times, I have even fasted for a month just on Sea Moss and water alone it was very nice but not tasty. Green Food Plus is very good also. Just THINK Seaweed must be a very tough plant. I don't think that I could live at the bottom of the sea or ocean with no light, heat, or oxygen and still survive and be strong fit as well, what about YOU?

4) **Turpentine**

Turpentine comes from the pine tree; it is very good for healing if the right dosage is used but it can be harmful if exceeded. I have heard many reports from the Caribbean Islands of people who have cured themselves of coronavirus using turpentine.

Please check out the next extract, it will explain a little more. Check out the full article when you get chance as it shows you how turpentine can be used to cure many illnesses:

> *"Turpentine has been used as a natural remedy for a variety of health problems for generations! Great-grandmothers used turpentine for a yearly "cleansing" for every member of the family or for her rheumatism and nagging cough. While the thought of using paintbrush cleaner sounds harsh and foolish, turpentine could be classified as a herbal remedy.*
>
> *Herbal remedies are medicines made from plants, and that is just what true turpentine is! Turpentine is made by distilling pine resin from pine trees. Many essential oils are made by distilling plant material into a concentrated natural medicine."*30

---

30 https://earthclinic.com/remedies/turpentine/ accessed April 7th 2020 @08:14

5) **Water**

We, humans, are water beings. When we are born, we come from the primordial waters. We are 70–80% water. We are also electric beings. To be fully optimized we really should be drinking a gallon (4.5 litres) of water every day. This would also assist to flush disease, parasites, and toxins from our bodies. I do not know one person who actually does this which is most worrying. It just pre-empts me to ask myself, how are we living and in WHO'S WAY?

6) **Immune Boosters**

- Vitamin C
- Hot teas (green, cinnamon, etc.)
- Elderberry and berries
- Broths and soups (preferably vegetable ones)
- Hot or boiling water (preferably mineral or spring water)
- Bell peppers (preferably raw)
- Spirulina
- Chlorella
- Neem powder
- Ginger (raw as possible, increase water intake
- Limes, lemons, papaya, and watermelons
- Honey
- Purple carrots
- Liquorice root
- Sunflower and pumpkin seeds
- Black cumin and turmeric powder
- Navy beans

7) **Herbs With High Iron Content**

- Sarsaparilla
- Burdock root

- Stinging nettle
- Hops
- Dandelion Greens
- Yellow dock root
- Kale
- Prunes
- Cayenne Pepper
- Oregano
- Basil
- Raspberry (fruit and leaves)
- Fennel
- Rhubarb root
- Black Walnut (nut & inner husks)
- Tamarind
- Dill
- Chaga
- Key Limes
- Ortigia
- Seeded gapes
- Sour orange hydrangea root
- Red clover
- Callaloo
- Thyme

8) Essential Oils

Essential oils in tea and the air are good for your immune system and for killing germs and bacteria. You can put it in a bowl of boiling water and put a cloth or towel over your head and use the vapour to cleanse your respiratory system (the steam will break up the mucus in your chest [eucalyptus and tea tree oil are good]).

61

9) Sage

Burn sage as it kills up to 94% of the bacteria within the air.

10) **Exercise**

Exercise is very important as OUR sweat removes toxicity from OUR bloodstreams.

11) **Fasting**

Many people do not know this, but fasting is excellent for healing and curing the body.

It is only fair that we hear from Dr Sebi, the master herbalist, who has cured people from all illnesses. Let US hear about his experiences with fasting:

> "Well me I like to fast because when I fast, I am better for her (points at wife). Because I'm healthier, like. My mother died the day I was coming here, I couldn't turn back because she would have liked that. So, I said I'm going to stop eating, but I ate last night with Linda and I'm not going to eat today, not going to eat tomorrow. I'm going to get back I told my wife we're going to stop eating for about two months because it's good. Twelve days is good. A

good fast, stop eating for twelve days every year and you drink plenty of water and plenty of juice, water and juice and that Green Food Plus.

It's going to cost you 49,95$, right? But you drink three in the morning that's all you need three capsules in the morning, and you go about your business. Because that's what I had today and I have a lot of energy right now, okay. You drink water and your juice, and you drink your Green Food Plus."

"Well, juice. I have tamarind juice in Honduras, but here you have apple juice. It's okay, it's not going to nourish you, but it's gonna prevent you from going into some sort of madness.

*So yes Lisa "Left Eye" Lopes when I met Lisa (hands shaking) and her eyes she blinks them really fast, said I need help. I said we all need help, me too. Five months later Lisa was talking to me and her eyes never blinked and her (steady hands), Lisa was nice. Lisa realized, Lisa fasted for 42 days and 42 nights. Lisa came to my hut at two o'clock in the morning. She came with these two mounds of **Sea Moss**. Oh, I'm glad I'm talking about **Sea Moss**.*

***Sea Moss** brothers and sisters, I drink Sea Moss every day and Lisa started drinking **Sea Moss** and she saw her body filling up and her nerves nice and she says, "I love you Dr Sebi", I said I love you more. She said, thank you, but you know what happened, right? Well, that's okay everything is in divine order."*

> *"In the morning I wake up she always has a mug of Sea Moss and that's it, and my three, I have an African formula and also the Green Food Plus and I'm gone, like right now, I'm gone. In the evening mmm... a salad, a little salad and I put my little onion salad dressing on it and I'm good to go. I feel good because my stomach is empty, but if my stomach was big, my back would be strained, my eyes would be bad, and everything would go bad. See we've been eating wrong and I have to thank messenger Elijah Muhammad.*
>
> *Messenger Elijah Muhammad is the only man that made the statement that they give us the wrong food to eat, listen carefully Elijah Muhammad said that. I sat and ate with the messenger 38/37 South Woodland Avenue at his table was John Ali Raymond Sharif. Myself and her and the messenger sitting at the opposite end of the table and I'm sitting at the other end. And the messenger cut me this meatloaf and he looking at us and he said "I want you all to know that the last thing to go in your mouth is this. And I hope that all of you would leave it soon one day."*[31]

You see, fasting is very important and should be incorporated in our lives, most of US are not aware of this FACT. Dr Sebi has always recommended that WE

---

31 https://www.naturalherbremedy.com/dr-sebi-the-benefits-of-fasting-and-sea-moss/ accessed April 8th 2020 @11:14

FAST at least 12 days a year (that is 12 days in a row). How many times have you ever fasted before and for how long? 1 day, 2 days, 3 days, 4? 5 days, 6 days, 7, days or more?

12) **Cut out junk food**

This speaks for itself.

13) **Cut out dairy products**

Dairy has also been proven to cause some minor discomfort like "low-grade inflammation or it may clog nasal passages.

14) **Cut out meat**

Cases of flu have been found in animals. We should be aware of this and exercise caution, that's not addressing the other problems which our consumption of meat causes.

15) **Cut out smoking and drinking**

Smoking and drinking damage your immune system.

16) **Cut out sugar**

Sugar intake reduces our energy; now is a time our bodies need to be fully optimized to keep our immune systems up.

17) **Positive thinking**

Our thoughts are the fastest traveling thing in the UNIVERSE, moving at 24 billion miles per second. They are very POWERFUL. Sometimes we have negative thoughts which make US ILL. This is called psychosomatic illness (the mind making the body sick). WHY don't WE use OUR MINDS to THINK POSITIVE for US to THINK and FEEL BETTER? How we THINK affects the way we FEEL, we can CHANGE and MANIFEST what WE want and APPLY it. One of the biggest killers today apart from vaccines is STRESS and ANXIETY.

18) **Weed**

Flavonoids and raw cannabinoids are known to kill germs and bacteria from inside our bodies. I am sure that it would assist in the case of COVID-19. But more research is needed in this area.

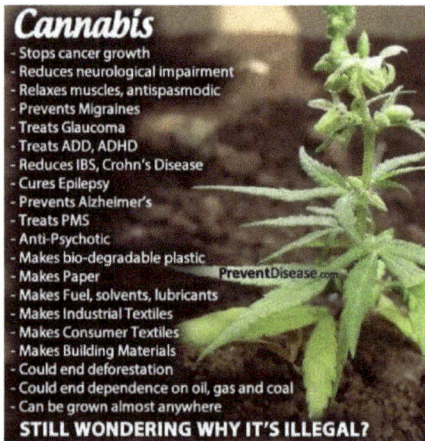

Cannabis
- Stops cancer growth
- Reduces neurological impairment
- Relaxes muscles, antispasmodic
- Prevents Migraines
- Treats Glaucoma
- Treats ADD, ADHD
- Reduces IBS, Crohn's Disease
- Cures Epilepsy
- Prevents Alzheimer's
- Treats PMS
- Anti-Psychotic
- Makes bio-degradable plastic
- Makes Paper
- Makes Fuel, solvents, lubricants
- Makes Industrial Textiles
- Makes Consumer Textiles
- Makes Building Materials
- Could end deforestation
- Could end dependence on oil, gas and coal
- Can be grown almost anywhere

PreventDisease.com

STILL WONDERING WHY IT'S ILLEGAL?

What do you think? Please check out the quote below:

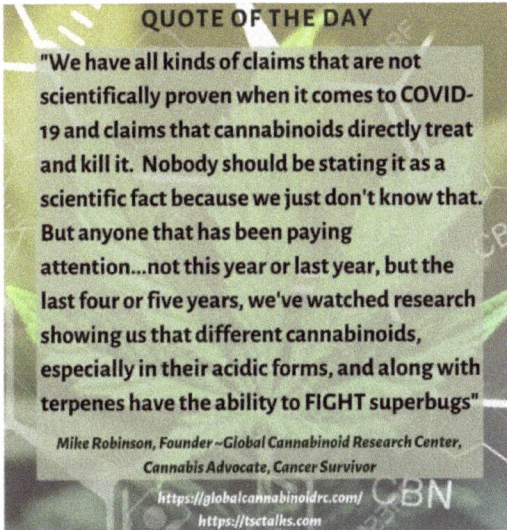

QUOTE OF THE DAY

"We have all kinds of claims that are not scientifically proven when it comes to COVID-19 and claims that cannabinoids directly treat and kill it. Nobody should be stating it as a scientific fact because we just don't know that. But anyone that has been paying attention...not this year or last year, but the last four or five years, we've watched research showing us that different cannabinoids, especially in their acidic forms, and along with terpenes have the ability to FIGHT superbugs"

Mike Robinson, Founder ~Global Cannabinoid Research Center, Cannabis Advocate, Cancer Survivor

https://globalcannabinoidrc.com/
https://tsctalks.com

Source: [32]

19) **Quinine**

Natural chloroquine, which comes from the bark of the Chinchona plant is good also. The natural stuff works better than synthetic.

20) **Sunlight**

Sunlight helps to boost our immune system as our body converts the sunlight into Vitamin D.

---

32 https://www.linkedin.com/posts/activity-6653722064912023552-ftys accessed April 9th 2020 @02:28

21) **Steam**

Take hot showers and hot baths, take deep breaths
(that will help break up the mucus).

UNNATURAL REMEDIES

1) **Interferon Alpha 2B (IFNrec)**

China, where the death rate peaked only a few weeks
ago at about 3%, is back to 0.7% – and rapidly
declining, while China is taking full control of the
disease – and that with the help of a not-spoken-
about medication developed 39 years ago by Cuba,
called "Interferon Alpha 2B (IFNrec)," very effective
for fighting viruses and other diseases, but is not
known and used in the world because the US under the
illegal embargo of Cuba does not allow the medication
to be marketed internationally.

2) **Chloroquine and hydroxychloroquine**

Chloroquine is an antimalaria drug. It is used to cure
malaria and is also used as a treatment for acute
malaria, it is usually given by injection.[33]
Hydroxychloroquine (HCQ), sold under the brand
name Plaquenil among others, is a medication used to

---

[33]
> https://web.archive.org/web/20151208200339/http://ww
> w.drugs.com/monograph/aralen-phosphate.html accessed
> April 9th 2020 @15:09

prevent and treat malaria in areas where malaria remains sensitive to chloroquine. Other uses include treatment of rheumatoid arthritis, lupus, and porphyria cutanea tarda. It is taken orally.

Dr Shiva Ayyadurai, MIT PhD economic and immune prescription to the president of America.

By now you must know Dr. Shiva. He made a shocking revelation in the video link in chapter 3. He proffered a 3-step solution that will deliver a solution to the economic and immune health for Americans.

Step 1 was to organize US citizens into 4 groups.

Step 2 was to deliver a personalized protocol for each group.

Step 3 was maintenance and back to work.

Whether President Trump listens, who knows?

For the full letter to the President of the United States read:

https://shiva4senate.com/immune-and-economic-health-for-america-coronavirus/

I have heard reports from the Caribbean, Africa, and China that many people who have been using these remedies are highlighted successfully to cure themselves of coronavirus (COVID-19). But I have also heard that regulatory bodies including the WHO advise that clinical trials are necessary before it can be readily accepted and approved as a drug to eliminate or clear COVID-19. Even though people are dying a lot and this drug is saving people. Some things do not make sense. This drug has been approved in many countries for the treatment of malaria but at the moment it is deemed unsafe for COVID-19 as it hasn't been tested enough? What is going on?

Please check out the next extract:

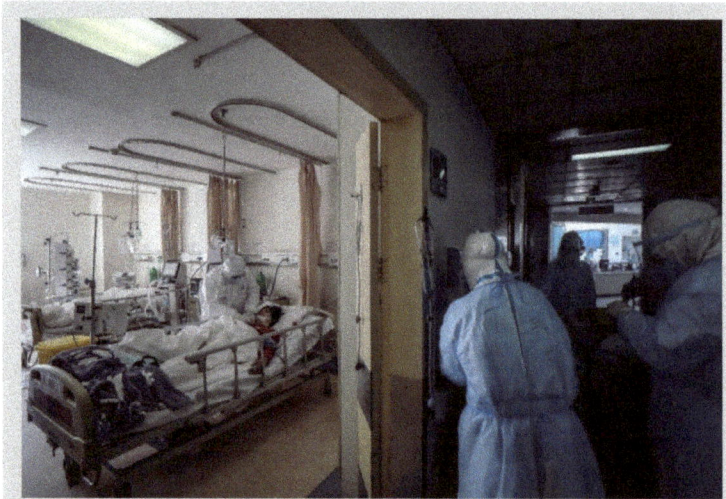

"Chinese experts, based on the result of clinical trials, have confirmed that chloroquine phosphate, an antimalarial drug, has a certain curative effect on the novel coronavirus disease (COVID-19), a Chinese official said on Monday.

The experts have "unanimously" suggested the drug be included in the next version of the treatment guidelines and applied in wider clinical trials as soon as possible, Sun Yanrong, deputy head of the China National Center for Biotechnology Development under the Ministry of Science and Technology (MOST), said at a press conference.

Chloroquine phosphate, which has been used for more than 70 years, was selected from tens of thousands of existing drugs after multiple rounds of screening, Sun said. According to her, the drug has been under clinical trials in over 10 hospitals in Beijing, as well as in south China's Guangdong Province and central China's Hunan Province, and has shown fairly good efficacy.

In the trials, the groups of patients who had taken the drug have shown better indicators than their parallel groups, in abatement of fever, improvement of CT images of lungs, the percentage of patients who became negative in viral nucleic acid tests and the time they need to do so, she said.

Patients taking the drug also take a shorter time to recover, she added. Sun gave an example of a 54-year-old patient in Beijing, who was admitted to hospital four days after showing symptoms. After taking the drug for a week, he saw all indicators improve and the nucleic acid turn negative.

So far, no obvious serious adverse reactions related to the drug have been found among the over 100 patients enrolled in the clinical trials, she said. On

Feb. 15, *several departments including the MOST, the National Health Commission and the National Medical Products Administration called a video conference to listen to drug research and clinical experts' opinions on the drug's efficacy on COVID-19.*

The expert team, led by Zhong Nanshan, a renowned respiratory specialist and an academician of the Chinese Academy of Engineering, agreed that chloroquine phosphate can be used to treat more COVID-19 patients, Sun said.

Previous in vitro experiments showed that it can block virus infections by changing the acidity and basicity value inside the cell and interfering receptors of SARS coronavirus. It also shows immune-modulating activity, which may enhance its antiviral effect in vivo and is widely distributed in the whole body, including the lungs, after oral administration." 34

---

34 https://www.thejakartapost.com/life/2020/02/20/
    antimalarial-drug-confirmed-effective-on-covid-19-
    chinese-official.html   accessed April 9th 2020 @15:11

Please check out the next extract. It fills in a few gaps:

> "*Chloroquine for COVID-19: Cutting Through the Hype*
>
> *President Donald Trump has touted the drug as a treatment, but scientists still don't know for sure that it is effective in patients. A number of clinical trials aim to find out.*
>
> *On March 16, SpaceX founder <u>Elon Musk tweeted</u> that the anti-malaria drug chloroquine was "maybe worth considering" as a treatment for COVID-19. He got 13,000 retweets. By March 19, President Donald Trump was touting chloroquine at a press conference. He even announced that the Food and Drug Administration had fast-tracked its approval for COVID-19. The FDA <u>denied that this was the case</u> a short time later.*
>
> *While some of the hype has been fuelled by <u>a document</u> generated outside the scientific literature, chloroquine's potential in treating COVID-19 is gaining traction in the medical community.*
>
> *The drug has a long track record in medicine, having been used since the 1940s as an antimalarial. The modern drug is a synthetic form of quinine, which is found in the bark of the Cinchona plant. The plant was taken as a herbal remedy by indigenous Peruvians four centuries ago to treat fever. And there*

are some early indications it could work against SARS-CoV-2 infections.

There's often a huge gap between how it works in the lab cells and how it works in the body.

— Jeremy Rossman, University of Kent

For instance, a study in France published on March 20 in the *International Journal of Antimicrobial Agents* described the treatment of 42 patients hospitalized with COVID-19, 26 of whom received a version of chloroquine called hydroxychloroquine and 16 of whom received routine care. Of the 20 patients who took the antimalarial and completed the study, six also received azithromycin, an antibiotic. All six of these patients were free of SARS-CoV-2 by the fifth-day post-treatment, while seven of 14 patients who took hydroxychloroquine alone were negative for the virus, and two of 16 control patients were no longer infected.

Small-scale experiments in which chloroquine has been given to COVID-19 patients in China and Australia have also shown encouraging results as far as shortening the course of the disease.

Larger clinical trials will be necessary to determine how effective the drug is. Researchers at the University of Minnesota have embarked on a study including 1,500 people to probe the drug's effectiveness further in preventing the development of COVID-19 after people are exposed to SARS-CoV-2. The results could be available in a matter of weeks, Jakub Tolar, the dean of the University of Minnesota Medical School and vice president for clinical affairs, tells <u>Reuters</u>, and might indicate whether it's worth launching a larger trial.

A small trial of 1,500 people would be a pragmatic step towards verifying the drug's efficacy, says <u>Jeremy Rossman</u>, a virologist at the University of Kent, who praises the approach.

A number of other chloroquine experiments on humans are in the works. According to clinicaltrials.gov, researchers at the University of Oxford plan to give it as a <u>prophylactic</u> to 10,000 health care workers and others at high risk of contracting SARS-CoV-2. In <u>Norway</u>, doctors expect to begin administering the drug to hospitalized patients. And in Thailand, clinicians are preparing for a clinical trial comparing <u>various combinations of antivirals</u>, including chloroquine.

Chloroquine's mechanism of action

If chloroquine is shown to be effective against SARS-CoV-2, it will not be via the same mechanism by which the drug functions as an antimalarial. That's because malaria is caused not by a virus but by a microparasite of the Plasmodium genus. Chloroquine makes it toxic for the parasite to digest its host's hemoglobin.

Chloroquine might have entirely different effects against a virus, such as, for example, disrupting the virus's ability to enter a cell. 35

It's funny, we are locked down, in a state of emergency. People are panicking everywhere all stressed and anxious. People are dying everywhere, which is heartbreaking to see. And when we look into things closely, we realize that most of the people are dying for reasons other than COVID-19. Of course, some are dying of COVID-19 but not as many as they say. When you look into things closely you will see other anomalies under the surface. Some we have already spoken of. Big pharma is just a BULLYING CARTEL that puts profits over lives.

76

"Profit over lives is not very nice"

– Kwadw(o) Naya: Baa Ankh Em Ra A'lyun Eil

In these situations, we need to find and stick to what works.

I have known of this drug, have known it for years, I know people who have taken it many times to cure the

---

35 https://www.the-scientist.com/news-opinion/is-hype-over-chloroquine-as-a-potential-covid-19-therapy-justified--67301 accessed April 9th 2020 @15:41

flu and malaria and they swear by it. If the right dosage is taken it does not appear to be harmful at all, but it can be slightly toxic if overdosed. I will let one of my friends make a testimony at the end of this section to explain in his words how it went.

Chloroquine and hydroxychloroquine are cheap to make, they could rapidly (with ease), be rolled out across the world to slow down or even eradicate this pandemic. But WHO and other regulatory bodies deem it unsafe and are demanding clinical trials? Do you know how many innocent healthy people die in these clinical trials?! They really don't highlight this side, do they?

Both hydroxychloroquine and chloroquine have been approved as safe and effective drugs to treat malaria but are not deemed safe for COVID-19 even though many people have used it over the last three months and have been cured. I don't get it, do you? And guess what? Who do you think is involved with the clinical trials which are being proposed? I will give you one guess. I am sure that you will get it straight away... No other than Mr Bill Gates, the good old philanthropist, whatever one of those is.

77

Bill Gates believes that investing in research at scale and speed is the only way to find out for sure whether these drugs can help in this pandemic. As part of the COVID-19 Therapeutics Accelerator, an initiative was launched by welcome, The Bill and Melinda Gates Foundation and Mastercard funded them also.

I will let you hear the testimonial before moving on to the next solution.

Over to Eddy:

> *"Chloroquine is a drug used to treat malaria and basically fevers majority of Africans whom have lived on the continent and fallen ill of Malaria have had chloroquine administered to them and healed afterwards of malaria without side effects, however when it's injected depending on the individual, some persons do have side effects, such as itching, heavy sweating, loss of appetite and shivering's at night for possibly 4 days and when asked I was told that it was due to chloroquine pulling out the disease and boosting the human immune system to attack the disease.*
>
> *I personally have had chloroquine on several occasions both the injection as well as the tablets hydroxychloroquine which are an upgraded version from the chloroquine injections.*
>
> *Hydroxy chloroquine tablets seem to be not as harsh as the injections and patients usually have lesser reactions to hydroxychloroquine such as the itchy sensation is reduced, shivering E. T. C depending on the patient. However, both are very much used till date, it's a matter of the patients' preference, how they react to both and medical practitioners discretion if it's best to administer chloroquine*

injections or take hydroxychloroquine tablets for the treatment of malaria.

Chloroquine is so rampant and readily available in most African countries that pharmacist administer chloroquine injections for their patients to save time and costs of going to hospitals for a doctor or nurse to administer chloroquine injections.

Edward Afriking Vii Dauda April 13th 2020 @ 11:53

3) Liquid vitamin IV Vitamin Drip

This is a vitamin drip that provides our bodies with instant immune-boosting protection. Doctors say that **liquid Vitamin C**, via an **IV** or multiple injections, can **cure** coronavirus patients near death. Experienced health professionals feel that the masks will not prevent you from getting the virus or any virus because viruses are usually too small for masks to work.

For legal reasons, physicians are often restricted in the amount that they can inject in a patient, for whatever reason, they are usually not permitted to inject more than 1000 mg of Vitamin C into a patient. This could be the difference between life and death. You see, if they could have injected the patient 1000mg per 1 kilogram of body weight, the patient would naturally recover faster, because that is how vitamin C works.

Doctors say that high doses of liquid Vitamin C prevent any virus from getting into a normal human cell. During this COVID-19 CRISIS, vitamin C has been given to patients globally via liquid vitamin IV with a great deal of success.

4)   Z-pack

Z-pack is antibiotic **azithromycin**, it is also known as a potential treatment for COVID-19. Reportedly it has been used to much success during this current crisis. It is often used in conjunction with hydro chloroquine.

There are so many solutions both real and synthetic, solutions that actually work. I have gone through a few here so you can get the idea, but when you start researching you will see more.

As mentioned, personally speaking, I like to only deal with natural substances, but it is each to their own. As long as we cure the disease and not treat the symptoms, we will be ok. But in hindsight, prevention is better than cure. With that in MIND, we must keep our bodies and immune system in tip-top shape.

I have looked at today's coronavirus statistics for people dying of coronavirus in the UK and the US and it's very worrying. In China, people are getting cured. In the US and the UK, I feel sorry for you. I do not know what is happening here, but more people seem to be dying than surviving in these two countries?

From Thursday 9th to Wednesday 15th, the MEDIA in the UK have already predicted 900 deaths. **Imagine that? This makes no sense to me. Well, no common sense.** Unless someone is benefitting from this scenario? Or unless there are hidden (occult) agendas. **Black ops?**

What about the situation with the testing kits? There are various ways of testing the virus, most are either molecular or serological tests. The medical news today described it like this:

Molecular tests

Molecular tests look for signs of an active infection. They usually involve taking a sample from the back of the throat with a cotton swab. It is then sent to the lab for testing. The sample will undergo what is called polymerase chain reaction (PCR) test. This type of test is designed to detect signs of the virus's genetic material.

A PCR test can confirm a diagnosis of COVID-19 if it identifies two specific SARS-CoV-2 genes. If it identifies only one of these genes, it will produce an inconclusive result. Molecular tests can only help diagnose current cases of COVID-19. They cannot tell whether someone has had the infection and since recovered.

Serological tests

Serological tests detect antibodies that the body produces to fight the virus. These antibodies are present in anyone who has recovered from COVID-19. The antibodies exist in blood and tissues throughout the body. The test usually requires a blood sample. Serological tests are particularly useful for detecting cases of infection with mild or no symptoms.

The Centers for Disease Control and Prevention (CDC) are currently developing a serological test for SARS-CoV-2 and they are looking for blood samples from anyone who has had COVID-19. The samples would be taken at least 21 days after symptoms first developed.

Now, these are the two major ways to test.

But how can we test people with inefficient, inadequate testing kits that give faulty readings?

This still baffles me today.

Some people claim that coronavirus is new so doctors find it hard to accurately interpret the results. Even when someone tests negative but has symptoms it's advised you still quarantine yourself.

"If you have had likely exposures and symptoms suggest Covid-19 infection, you probably have it — even if your test is negative," wrote Harlan Krumholz, a professor of medicine at Yale, in The New York Times.

Catherine Klapperich, Director of the Laboratory for Diagnostics and Global Healthcare Technologies at Boston University believes that health care providers and patients don't have the information they need to have their test results correctly diagnosed with 100% accuracy.

Name me one accurate test?

Name me one consistent test?

Before we had the PCR test which is known to be 80.33% inaccurate as tests have shown, there are another two tests which are being carried out now. Rather you than me!

People cure themselves naturally time and time again, but when they go to a hospital then it is a whole different ball game. Often, they do not come out! We feel sorry for health professionals out there trying their best. But having to work with low budgets, inefficient training and equipment, poor conditions, it must be hard for them. Imagine being a Doctor and someone comes in with an illness that the government says that there is no cure for? That there is no equipment to even deal with it, no masks, medication, nothing.

No wonder people are dying.

If this is LIFE it is no life.

CHAPTER 5

WHY SHOULD I NOT HAVE THE COVID-19 VACCINE?

Because YOU MAY **DIE!**

Strange...but, **TRUE!**

Even if you have FLU like symptoms, it is most advisable **NOT** to have any **VACCINATIONS** as the **VACCINATIONS** could **KILL** YOU! If you have FLU like symptoms, it is most advisable, that you TAKE FLU LIKE MEDICINE PREFERABLY NATURAL. CURE BY NATURAL NATURE is always the BEST WAY. **UNNATURAL MEDICINES** tend to TREAT OUR SYMPTOMS but they do not usually CURE us of the ROOT **DISEASE or ILLNESS!**

If YOU TAKE the VACCINE YOU MAY WELL BE IN **TROUBLE**. The coronavirus is in the **VACCINE**, not in the SYMPTOMS. If you don't **KNOW** this, I suggest you check it OUT.

But before we do, let me tell you about Dr Stanley Plotkin who came out clean about the vaccinations, diseases and more that he has either created or participated in placing them upon innocent people. Here is the video.

https://www.youtube.com/watch?v=GhzXTaen9Uk&feature=share

Here is a comment by a viewer:

"Now think of these human aborted fetal tissue cells being directly injected into our tissues and bloodstream. This new DNA is combining with our own DNA which leads to mutations in our cells. Replicating over months or years. Illness and disease begin to set in like cancer, diabetes, autoimmune diseases, seizures, etc. It's not just about foreign DNA but the other toxins like aluminium, formaldehyde, polysorbates, Mercury, animal cells are also causing genetic mutations within us. Scientists are only beginning to study and understand epigenetics. Just like fingerprints, each persons' DNA is unique and vaccines is not a one size fits all medicine. As every vaccine insert, CDC and vaccine manufacturer state vaccines are NOT tested long term, for carcinogenic or mutagenic properties as well as infertility. Say NO to vaccines until further truthful research can be done while also cleaning up they're ingredients."

Now let us start with the etymology of vaccine.

WHAT is a **VACCINE**? HOW does it WORK?

Did YOU KNOW that they will start TESTING PEOPLE who come forward portraying or displaying FLU like SYMPTOMS and many, many people will come UP POSITIVE with coronavirus due to the inadequacies, inaccuracies, and inconsistencies with the testing equipment. It is true, their testing equipment, procedures and standards are ALL DEBATABLE. How is it possible for US to KNOW and BE AWARE of this FACT if WE do not EVEN KNOW how VACCINES WORK?

87

Let US LOOK into the definitions:

<u>VACCINE</u>

noun <u>[Countable or Uncountable]</u>

UK /ˈvæk.siːn/

US /ˈvæk.siːn/

A <u>substance</u> <u>containing</u> a <u>virus</u> or <u>bacterium</u> in a <u>form</u> that is not <u>harmful</u>, given to a <u>person</u> or <u>animal</u> to <u>prevent</u> them from getting the <u>disease</u> that the <u>virus</u> or <u>bacterium</u> <u>causes</u>:

This vaccine protects against some kinds of bacteria.[36]

VACCINATE

verb [Transitive]

/ˈvæk.sɪ.neɪt/ us

/ˈvæk.sə.neɪt/

To give someone a vaccine, usually by injection, to prevent them from getting a disease:

The children were vaccinated against the major childhood diseases.

See also

inoculate

immunize specialized [37]

---

36 https://dictionary.cambridge.org/dictionary/english/vaccine accessed March 28th 2020 @11:59

37
    https://dictionary.cambridge.org/dictionary/english/vaccinate accessed March 28th 2020 @12:07

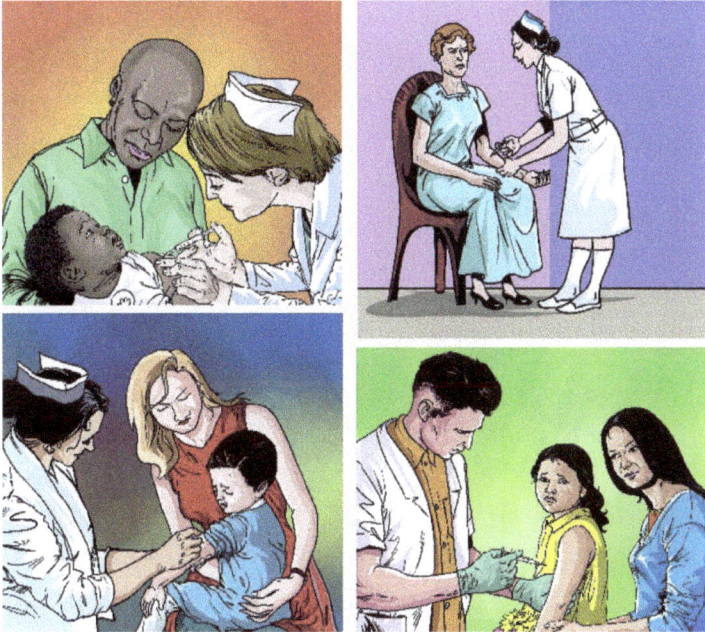

As WE CAN SEE, vaccinations do not make sense. Why would WE have someone inject a disease or virus inside our bodies to CURE it, (albeit non-harmful)? WE have heard it all. Stop and THINK about it PLEASE. It sounds like they would like US to get VACCINATED with DISEASE(S) to TREAT OUR SYMPTOMS. Very nice people, very nice world, NOT. It is plain for all to SEE!

Why would anyone want a weakened or killed virus injected in them? Please tell me why anyone would do this? Especially when there are always plenty of natural/holistic CURES out there. Not just TREATMENTS (which will have one coming back time and time again until they drop out early).

I have my own vaccine. It's called my IMMUNE SYSTEM and I've been caring for it for years. Maybe it would be better for people to focus on optimizing their own IMMUNE SYSTEM, as opposed to receiving VACCINES. Maybe that would be a better way to go? Or maybe I am CRAZY? I will let YOU decide on this one.

Soon they will be wanting and attempting to get everyone to TEST for COVID-19 with dodgy testing kits which will show many, many, unassuming innocents as positive when they are, in fact, negative. This will cause a national state of emergency, increased restrictions and more power to government and law agents, decreasing OUR LIBERTIES and FREEDOMS. Is this WHAT WE REALLY WANT? REALLY? And how would WE KNOW if this were to happen or not?

But if you LOOK deep into things you may SEE that ALL is not as it SEEMS. Or ALL could be NORMAL. It is ALL down to perception (individual or group). I am AWARE of my PERCEPTION concerning these MATTERS. Are you AWARE of YOURS? Or do YOU USUALLY TEND to GO ALONG with the POPULAR RHETORIC? They say PEOPLE are SHEEPLE. It is even in OUR dictionaries now.

Please read the next comments, I stumbled across them online:

> " 🌍Listen carefully! - NONE of this is an accident.
> Almost ANYONE can "Test positive" for the #covid19.

> *It is simply the plan being successfully played out as the script was written for it to do so. Farrakhan has been teaching this for over 50 YEARS ☺ They CREATE the "problem", they KNOW it will cause a REACTION then they magically "provide" the "SOLUTION" which will be; **1. vaccines. 2. R.F.I.D chips instead of cash** to control everything we do just like Sweden. **3. Pharmaceutical drugs. 4. #depopulation** - Plain & simple. We must become aware, and awake, then refuse this! They intend to use this #coronaSCARE to destroy the economy and usher in a new economic system which is fully electronic and controlled by them. NO CASH, just electronic currency controlled through an R.F.I.D system......"*
>
> - Rizza Islam [38]

Extreme and shocking views but I tend to agree with the author here. What are YOUR THOUGHTS about these AFFAIRS? They will soon be encouraging people to test for COVID-19. If I were YOU, I most definitely would not put myself forward for this. WHY? Because they could KILL ME. MARK ME FOR GENOCIDE. YOU THINK that I am just chatting like some 'chatty patty', please look into these matters for YOURSELF.

---

[38]

https://www.facebook.com/rizzaislam1/videos/1440269 83659803/ accessed March 28th 2020 @13:18

The tests that they are USING are 40+-year-old tests which they have used in the past for detecting HIV and AIDS. But it is only around 80% inaccurate. This has been proven time and time again. Why would one even want to put themselves forward for one of these tests? Yet many will be RUSHING for the VACCINES and the TEST. If anything happens to those people, don't say that I did not warn YOU.

Rather than just take it from me, it is best if you hear from some people a lot more KNOWLEDGED and EXPERIENCED in these affairs.

First, let us hear from Phil Valentine, he has done some excellent research into the COVID-19 pandemic.

> *"The Polymere Chain Reaction, or ["PCR test"], has been around for at least 40 years – and was found to be 80.33% inaccurate ... Rendering False Positives as well as False Negatives. This test was part of the testing models for HIV, and was assumed to detect "individual viruses"... But was found to be susceptibly hyper-sensitive to being corrupted by surrounding environmental materials."*
>
> *– Phil Valentine.*

It is not just talk either, you can see for yourself:

Potential False-Positive Rate Among the 'Asymptomatic Infected Individuals' in Close Contacts of COVID-19 Patients

G H Zhuang [1] , M W Shen, L X Zeng, B B Mi, F Y Chen, W J Liu, L L Pei, X Qi, C Li

Abstract

Objective: As the prevention and control of COVID-19 continues to advance, the active nucleic acid test screening in the close contacts of the patients has been carrying out in many parts of China. However, the false-positive rate of positive results in the screening has not been reported up to now. But to clarify the false-positive rate during screening is important in COVID-19 control and prevention.

Method: Point values and reasonable ranges of the indicators which impact the false-positive rate of positive results were estimated based on the information available to us at present. The false-positive rate of positive results in the active screening was deduced, and univariate and multivariate-probabilistic sensitivity analyses were performed to understand the robustness of the findings.

Results: When the infection rate of the close contacts and the sensitivity and specificity of reported results were taken as the point estimates, the positive predictive value of the active screening was only 19.67%, in contrast, the false-positive rate of positive results was 80.33%. The multivariate-probabilistic sensitivity analysis results supported the base-case findings, with a 75% probability for the false-positive rate of positive results over 47%.

Conclusions: In the close contacts of COVID-19 patients, nearly half or even more of the 'asymptomatic infected individuals' reported in the active nucleic acid test screening might be false positives.

Keywords: COVID-19; Close contacts; False-positive; Nucleic acid test; Screening." [39]

Please check out the next extract also:

"**Mail**Online

Mother-of-two, 34, claims she was left blind, diagnosed with multiple sclerosis, and covered in a rash 'after having the FLU JAB' and fears she may never recover

- *Jennifer Whitney, 34, was diagnosed with MS just weeks after her flu shot*

- *She was forced by boss to have the shot, then sacked for taking time off work*

- *Symptoms included her hair falling out, blisters all over her face and body*

- *The mother-of-two was also left blind for 10 months and unable to conceive*

39 https://pubmed.ncbi.nlm.nih.gov/32133832/ accessed April 5th 2020

- Doctors confirmed her immune system was attacking her brain and nerves

- A naturopath believes the MS was likely to have been caused by the vaccine

95

Jennifer Whitney, from Mukilteo, Washington, had the vaccine due to the insistence of her boss - despite being concerned about any side effects.

By Jacqui Deevoy For Mailonline

Published: 22 December 2017

You can check out the full article at the link below. [40]

Next, I would like us to hear from a worker in the healthcare field. This was originally taken from a medical forum. The author wishes to stay anonymous because presenting any narrative different to the official could cause a lot of stress within the toxic environment in which they find themselves working – caused by the COVID-19 scam.

Did I just say that it was a scam? What are YOUR THOUGHTS?

Kindly check the next article, it is a little long but well worth the read:

> *"I work in the healthcare field. Here's the problem, we are testing people for any strain of a coronavirus. Not specifically for COVID-19. There are no reliable tests for a specific COVID-19 virus. There are no reliable agents or media outlets for reporting numbers of actual COVID-19 virus cases. This needs*

---

40 https://www.dailymail.co.uk/health/article-5205097/Mother-34-claims-flu-vaccine-destroyed-life.html?fbclid=IwAR0dFljDc-OuY5wkCjTygAXIGnpZc38ySt-KFKbtz8iblRrI--KzjnBri6I accessed March 30th 2020 @20:33

to be addressed first and foremost. Every action and reaction to COVID-19 is based on totally flawed data and we simply cannot make accurate assessments. This is why you are hearing that most people with COVID-19 are showing nothing more than cold/flu-like symptoms. That is because most Coronavirus strains are nothing more than cold/flu-like symptoms. The few actual novel Coronavirus cases do have some worse respiratory responses, but still have a very promising recovery rate, especially for those without prior issues.

The 'gold standard' in testing for COVID-19 is laboratory isolated/purified coronavirus particles free from any contaminants and particles that look like viruses but are not, that have proven to be the cause of the syndrome known as COVID-19 and obtained by using proper viral isolation methods and controls (not the PCR that is currently being used or Serology/antibody tests which do not detect virus as such). PCR basically takes a sample of your cells and amplifies any DNA to look for 'viral sequences', i.e. bits of non-human DNA that seems to match parts of a known viral genome.

The problem is the test is known not to work. It uses 'amplification' which means taking a very very tiny amount of DNA and growing it exponentially until it can be analysed. Obviously, any minute contaminations in the same sample will also be amplified leading to potentially gross errors of discovery.

Additionally, it's only looking for partial viral sequences, not whole genomes, so identifying a single pathogen is next to impossible even if you ignore the other issues.

The Mickey Mouse test kits being sent out to hospitals, at best, tell analysts you have some viral DNA in your cells. Which most of us do, most of the time. It may tell you the viral sequence is related to a specific type of virus – say the huge family of coronavirus. But that's all. The idea these kits can isolate a specific virus-like COVID-19 is nonsense. And that's not even getting into the other issue – viral load.

If you remember the PCR works by amplifying minute amounts of DNA. It therefore is useless at telling you how much virus you may have. And that's the only question that really matters when it comes to diagnosing illness. Everyone will have a few viruses kicking around in their system at any time, and most will not cause illness because their quantities are too small. For a virus to sicken you need a lot of it, a massive amount of it. But PCR does not test viral load and therefore can't determine if an osteogenesis is present in sufficient quantities to sicken you. If you feel sick and get a PCR test any random virus DNA might be identified even if they aren't all involved in your sickness which leads to false diagnosis.

And coronavirus are incredibly common. A large percentage of the world human population will have covi DNA in them in small quantities even if they are perfectly well or sick with some other pathogen. Do you see where this is going yet? If you want to create a totally false panic about a totally false pandemic – pick a coronavirus.

They are incredibly common and there's tons of them. A very high percentage of people who have become sick by other means (flu, bacteria, pneumonia, anything) will have a positive PCR test for covi even if you're doing them properly and ruling out contamination, simply because covis are so common.

There are hundreds of thousands of flu and pneumonia victims in hospitals throughout the world at any one time.

*All you need to do is select the sickest of these in a single location – say Wuhan – administer PCR test to them and claim anyone showing viral sequences similar to a coronavirus (which will inevitably be quite a few) is suffering from a 'new' disease. Since YOU ALREADY SELECTED THE SICKEST FLU CASES A FAIRLY HIGH PROPORTION OF YOUR SAMPLE WILL GO ON TO **DIE**.*

You can then say this 'new' virus has a CFR higher than the flu and use this to infuse more concern and do more tests which will of course produce more 'cases', which expands the testing, which produces yet more 'cases' and so on and so on.

Before long, you have your 'pandemic', and all you have done is use a simple test kit trick to convert the worst flu and pneumonia cases into something new that doesn't actually exist.

Now just run the same scam in other countries. Making sure to keep the **FEAR MESSAGE** running high so that people will feel panicky and less able to think critically.

Your only problem is going to be that – due to the fact that there is no actual new deadly pathogen but just regular sick people, you are mislabelling your case numbers, and especially your DEATHS, are going to be way too low for a real deadly virus pandemic.

But you can stop people pointing this out in several ways:

1. You can claim this is just the beginning and more deaths are imminent. Use this as an excuse to quarantine everyone and then claim the quarantine prevented the expected millions of dead.

2. You can tell people that 'minimising' the dangers is irresponsible and bully them into not talking about numbers.

3.   *You can talk crap about made up numbers hoping to blind people with pseudoscience.*

4.   *You can start testing well people (who, of course, will also likely have shreds of coronavirus DNA in them) and thus inflate your 'case figures' with 'asymptomatic carriers' (you will of course have to spin that to sound deadly even though any virologist knows the more symptom-less cases you have the less deadly is your pathogen.*

Take these 4 simple steps and you can have your own entirely manufactured pandemic up and running in weeks.

They cannot "confirm" something for which there is no accurate test."

Please note Jaclyn Dunne's response to this:

"I said exactly this! They have picked a common pathogen that many people carry. It could have been adenovirus but too many know this is relatively harmless, it could have been streptococcus, again another common one, it could have been grippe.... Many, many people carry these at an active or sub active level. Particularly if they have asthma, a high dairy diet, past history of throat infections, chest infections.... The list is endless."

NEED WE SAY ANYMORE THAN THIS? From this PERSPECTIVE it LOOKS like a very EVIL SCAM indeed. ABUSE, TORTURE, and MASS GENOCIDE. WHAT DO YOU SAY?

Just one more thing.

Did you know that in 2009, Baxter International Inc, a Fortune 500 American health care company with headquarters in Deerfield, Illinois, was "unintentionally" caught red-handed distributing Influenza vaccines - 72 KG - containing live H5N1 avian flu viruses to EIGHTEEN different countries? [41]

Upon discovering both H5N1, and the human form, H3N2, in what should have been flu vaccines, the National Microbiology Laboratory in Canada thwarted the efforts of Baxter International by alerting the World Health Organization. It is not the first time this company has been involved in incidents like this. They knowingly sent infected HIV needles to Brazil! They also supplied the Third Reich with supplies during World War 2 which shows the longevity of the company.

During this time, they have carried out many violations, ranging from false claims and related environmental and nuclear safety violations, and well over $500 million in penalties. Why is this company still in business? Why

---

41 https://www.infowars.com/vaccines-as-biological-weapons-live-avian-flu-virus-placed-in-baxter-vaccine-materials-sent-to-18-countries/ accessed April 2nd 2020 @03:42

didn't we know about all this genocide and crimes against humanity which has been covertly administered on an international basis? Can you tell me?

One more question.

Are you going to take the vaccine for COVID-19? I would just like to check out a couple of images, I would be interested to know your thoughts.

They Plan to Kill People Using 5G, the Chip, Chemtrails, Vaccines all working together.

This Article is from an Unknown Source. Believe or Not!

The Chinese were all given mandatory vaccines last fall. The vaccine contained replicating, DIGITIZED (controllable) RNA which were activated by 60Ghz mm 5G waves that were just turned on in Wuhan (as well as all other Countries using 60Ghz 5G) with the "smart dust" that everyone on the globe has been inhaling through chemtrails. That's why when they say someone is "cured", the "virus" can be "digitally" reactivated at any time and the person can literally drop dead. [ ]The Diamond Princess Cruise ship was SPECIFICALLY equipped with 60Ghz 5G. It's basically remote assassination. Americans are currently breathing in this "smart" dust through chemtrails. Think of it like this..... add the combination of vaccines, chemtrails (smart dust) and 5G and your body becomes internally digitized and can be remotely controlled. A person's organ functions can be stopped remotely if one is deemed non-compliant. Wuhan was a test run for ID2020. The elite call this 60Ghz mm 5G wave the "V" wave (Virus) to mock us.   has created a space force in part to combat this weaponized technology. We need to vehemently REJECT the attempted "mandatory vaccine" issue because our lives depend on it.

This shows that a case has been filed to stop tech companies from being partners is a plan to kill people through technology.

Source: [42]

42 https://www.facebook.com/photo.php?fbid=2709762
119122794&set=a.607929932639367&type=3&theater&ifg=1
accessed April 5th 2020 @22:51

Case 3:19-cv-02407-CAB-AHG Document 1 Filed 12/16/19 PageID.2 **FILED**

Dec 16 2019

CLERK, U.S. DISTRICT COURT
SOUTHERN DISTRICT OF CALIFORNIA
BY _____ DEPUTY

1 Cyrus A. Parsa, The AI Organization
   4275 Executive Square Suite 200
2 La Jolla, California, 92037
   Phone Number (805-996-0135)
3 Email: Consult@theaiorganization.com

4

5 Cyrus A. Parsa, The AI Organization, PRO SE,

6

7   **UNITED STATES DISTRICT COURT SOUTHERN**

8   **DISTRICT OF CALIFORNIA**

9

10

11 The AI Organization, Inc, Cyrus A. Parsa, Victims of   ) Case No.: '19CV2407 CAB AHG
    Persecution, Rape, Torture, Concentration Camps,   )
12 Sex, Human and Organ Trafficking and Organ   )
    Harvesting in China, Hong Kong, America and Around   )
13 the World, not limited to democracy activists, Falun   ) COMPLAINT:
    Dafa Practitioners, Uyghurs, Christians, Tibetans,   )
14 Judges, Lawyers and Journalists tortured and killed in)
    China. John Does 1-Unlimited   )
15   )
              Plaintiff(s),   ) (1)MISUSE OF ARTIFICIAL
16   )   INTELLIGENCE, CYBERNETICS,
            vs.   )   ROBOTICS, BIOMETRICS,
17 Google L.L.C, Facebook Inc, DeepMind Inc, Alphabet   )   BIOENGINEERING, 5G AND
18 Inc, Neuralink Inc, Tesla Inc, Larry Page, Sergey Brin,)   QUANTUM COMPUTING
    Sundar Pichai, Mark Zuckerberg , Elon Musk, CISON   )   TECNNOLOGY
19 PR NewsWire & John Doe's 1-29   ) (2)ENDANGERING THE HUMAN
            Defendant(s).   )   RACE WITH THE MISUSE OF
20   )   ARTIFICAL INTELLIGENCE
21   )   TECHNOLOGY
22   ) (3)TRANSFER OF AI WEAPON
23   )   TECHNOLOGY TO CHINA
) (4)COMPLICTY IN GENOCIDE,
24   )   CHINA
25   (5)VIOLATION OF ARTICLE 1
                                                                 GENOCIDE CONVENTION
26   (6)VIOLATION OF ARTICLE 2
27   GENOCIDE CONVENTION,
                                                             (7)VIOLATION OF ARTICLE 3
28   GENOCIDE CONVENTION,

                              - 1 -
            INSERT DOCUMENT TITLE (e.g., MOTION TO STRIKE)

104

World Health Organization (WHO)

Q: Are vaccines safe?

A: Vaccines are safe. Any licensed vaccine is rigorously tested across multiple phases of trials before it is approved for use and continuously monitored to make sure it is safe and effective.

Vaccines are safe and effective.

Any licensed vaccine is rigorously tested before it is approved for use, regularly reassessed and constantly monitored for side effects. In the rare event a serious side effect is reported, it is immediately investigated.

World Health Organization

Source: 43

Please take a look at the next article, I don't know what to say really, most think that it is real but there is a small minority who say that it is fake. Then again, many people think that vaccines are safe including The World Health Organization (well, that is what they openly say in public). I will leave it to you to make up your own mind. I have left the full article, with references, it is only fair and right:

---

43 https://www.facebook.com/WHO/posts/2935886426456721 accessed April 13th @18:19

COVID-19 Vaccine Killed Seven Children in Senegal, Africa

By Alter Picar, April 9th, 2020

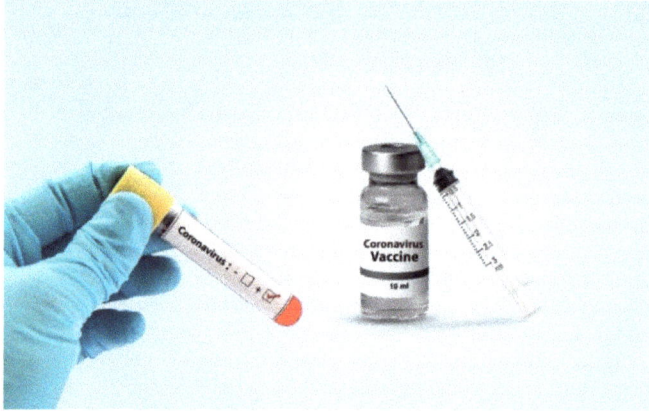

While some African leaders refused to test the COVID-19 vaccine on their country, the Senegal president allowed testing it on his people. The mass vaccination test already started this week and unfortunately, seven children who received the vaccine died immediately. It was reported that the people in charge of the process were now arrested and under the custody of the Senegal police for further investigation.

Meanwhile, a Youtube channel named, "Anggie's Fam," also confirmed this through a video that has been uploaded on April 6. In the video, the woman stated, *"Today, somebody called my husband; a nurse. A nurse told my husband that seven infants have died in Senegal due to this coronavirus vaccine. I just don't know why you must collect this thing when you know that it's not being tested? You want to use your people as guinea pigs or lab rats? Because of what? Do they give you money to kill? If you kill all your people in your land, who will remain to govern? You will end up going to the ground like you end up falling like zero level."*

She then continued, *"Let me tell you how this happened. This whole thing is in French but my husband speaks French so he understands everything and then he told me. Do you know that there's this guy, a Senegalese guy that went to this family in the village somewhere in Senegal trying to convince the family of seven kids?"* She went on to say that the man said, *"Oh let us give them the coronavirus vaccine, it's going to be well. Told them every sort of thing and trying to earn their trust. Then they gave him the consent to vaccinate the kids. Do you know what happened? All of them died, like almost immediately."*

107

On the other hand, two French doctors have sparked outrage after they discussed that Africa is the best destination to conduct tests for COVID-19 vaccine on live television. The video went viral and on social media where one of the doctors named Jean-Paul Mira proposed the idea of testing the vaccine on the African population. When some Africans learned about this, many of them strongly reacted and expressed their disapproval about the suggestion stating "You racist! Africa is not your playground!"

An individual on Twitter named Rim-Sarah Alouane, a PhD student and French researcher posted, *"This is horrific. Two French doctors on live television are discussing how a potential new treatment against COVID-19 should be first tested in Africa, "where no mask, no treatment, no reanimation, the same way experimental treatment for AIDS was done on prostitutes."*

This is not the first time that Africa has fallen victim to reckless and heartless medical experiments conducted by health institutions dominated by European and Western countries such as the World Health Organization (WHO). In 2014, Kenyan doctors found an anti-fertility agent in UN tetanus vaccine in a mass sterilization program. The *lifesitenews.com* reported this, with the excerpt saying, "This World Health Organization campaign is not about eradicating neonatal tetanus but a well-coordinated forceful population control mass sterilization exercise using a proven fertility regulating vaccine." Lifesitenews.com also stated that, "WHO's Kenyan office and several WHO media contacts in Washington, D.C. failed to respond to LifeSiteNews enquiries over a 24-hour period."

Meanwhile, on April 7, Business Insider also reported that "A potential coronavirus vaccine funded by Bill Gates is set to begin testing in people." It also proceeded by claiming, "Healthy volunteers in Philadelphia and Kansas City, Missouri, will begin to test an experimental coronavirus vaccine starting this week. The small Pennsylvania-based biotech Inovio Pharmaceuticals received regulatory clearance to begin testing. The Bill and Melinda Gates Foundation, along with other nonprofits, have poured funding into Inovio's vaccine project."

Bill Gates is one of the most influential people who can order mandates to WHO. If you ask why here is the reason. In a 2017 report, <u>politico.eu</u> stated, "*Over the past decade, the world's richest man has become the World Health Organization's second-biggest donor, second only to the United States and just above the United Kingdom. This largesse gives him outsized influence over its agenda, one that could grow as the U.S. and the U.K. threaten to cut funding if the agency doesn't make a better investment case.*"

In 2018, <u>modernghana.com</u> reported, "*Bill Gates has been showering vast sums of money on the World Health Organization (WHO), putting him in a position to shape its global infection disease policy and play a major role in the Ebola outbreak, it has emerged. In addition, the Gates Foundation gave up to US$ 75 million to an organization such as UNICEF and the International Federation of the Red Cross as well as to fund the development of Ebola vaccines.*

But these funds are small change compared to the 2 billion dollars that the Gates Foundation has given WHO between 1998 and 2014, making Bill Gates the second-largest donor after the USA."

109

References:

Coronavirus / COVID-19 vaccine deaths in Senegal
- https://ezone57.com/2020/04/08/coronavirus-covid-19-vaccine-killed-7-children-in-senegalwest-africa-video/

Video about the death of 7 children by Aggie's Fam
- https://www.youtube.com/watch?v=P_wYd9IAM3A&feature=share&

Video about the two French Doctors
- https://www.youtube.com/watch?v=NNqc77lTFGc

Kenyan doctors find anti-fertility agent in UN tetanus vaccine
- https://www.lifesitenews.com/news/a-mass-sterilization-exercise-kenyan-doctors-find-anti-fertility-agent-in-u

Meet the world's most powerful doctor: Bill Gates
- https://www.politico.eu/article/bill-gates-who-most-powerful-doctor/

Why Bill Gates Strongly Associated With The World Health Organization
- https://www.modernghana.com/news/856868/why-bill-gates-strongly-associated-with-the-world.html 44

---

44 https://web.archive.org/web/20200412225242/https://www.weblyf.com/author/alter/ accessed April 14th 2020 @08:16

I have my own mind; I will leave you to make up yours.

One more question!

Are you going to take the vaccine for COVID-19?

CHAPTER 6

WHO IS WHO?

Before we go into this, here is a poem by a young woman called, Sajj Liqbal.
https://mobile.facebook.com/story.php?story_fbid=10158399182415030&id=597465029&_rdr

"Who is the who?

Who is the who?

That told you what to do

Who or why did they tell you a lie?

Who is confused and refused the news

Who is Bill that wishes you ills to you and your family while making his plans?

Kwadw(o) Naya: Baa Ankh Em Ra A'lyun Eil

Vaccines is cure, his intentions are pure

Be wary otherwise thing turn scary, he wants to chip you like a dog so your movements are gone

It's all about readies just be careful, you don't turn into deadies

Walking around masked and gloved, bounded and subdued like a zombie

That isn't cool.

Now I respect my boundaries, and I know I am not a snub. I do my own research, I want to ask you.

Who is the who?

Who tells you what to do?

Is he the who or is it you?

Give me a clue.

So who's telling you guys what to do, that's what I am wanna know.

He has his windows and sells his computer tech.

Which somehow isn't his spec of a scientist who went testing to make a cure of a virus found on a floor, in the air and surfaces and basically, everywhere.

He couldn't cure windows but insist on curing you with the injection that pays him cash in a flash. A medicine of bioweapons to fill his pockets. It won't end there, it will be everywhere. Monies to be made. Billionaires.

I will stop the problem and of you, a quick and easy solution. I will get rich and you will die quick.

That is not Bill's concern because you are cheap and yes this is the end."

So that was the POEM but the WHO we are talking about in this chapter is the WORLD HEALTH ORGANIZATION. The World Health Organization (WHO), is a specialized agency of the United Nations which was founded in 1948 with a broad mandate to act as a coordinating authority on international health issues. Their main role is to further international cooperation for improved global health conditions. Their tasks include epidemic control, quarantine measures and drug standardization. This sounds all good and well until you have a LOOK 'underneath the bonnet.' As usual, all is not as it seems.

The WHO, under its constitution, defines health as "a state of complete physical, mental and social well-being, not just the absence of disease or infirmity." Committing to the promotion of the attainment of "the highest possible level of health." But do they? Let US take a LOOK.

The World Health Organization has declared the novel coronavirus outbreak a 'pandemic'. A pandemic is the worldwide spread of a new disease. Look at some of the major pandemics that have occurred since the 20th century... history is repeating itself.

If you're feeling under the weather at the moment and aren't sure whether it's the flu or coronavirus, this graphic from the World Health Organization is a really useful guide. If your symptoms match the symptoms for coronavirus then head to https://111.nhs.uk/covid-19.

https://www.facebook.com/timfarronmp/photos/a.377637175586623/3340526712630973/?type=3&theater accessed 2nd April 2020 @ 02:59

Symptoms	Coronavirus Symptoms range from mild to severe	Cold Gradual onset of symptoms	Flu Abrupt onset of symptoms
Fever	Common	Rare	Common
Fatigue	Sometimes	Sometimes	Common
Cough	Common* (usually dry)	Mild	Common* (usually dry)
Sneezing	No	Common	No
Aches and pains	Sometimes	Common	Common
Runny or stuffy nose	Rare	Common	Sometimes
Sore throat	Sometimes	Common	Sometimes
Diarrhea	Rare	No	Sometimes for children
Headaches	Sometimes	Rare	Common
Shortness of breath	Sometimes	No	No

Sources: World Health Organization, Centers for Disease Control and Prevention

The WHO does not have any power to force any country to work with them. Just like the CDC must work with local and state governments. If the CDC had the money to do its own surveillance and report freely on those findings we would not be here like this. We are not a third world country and thus should have had the mechanisms in place.

WHO's director-general Dr Tedros Ghebreyesus said the coronavirus outbreak is a greater risk to humanity than terrorism – newspunch.com. Yet, the World Health Organization (WHO) has refused to acknowledge the coronavirus treatment from Madagascar because "a vaccine is very unlikely to come from Africa," numerous international media have reported.

Madagascar stunned the world last week when President Andry Rajoelina launched the miracle "COVID-organics" - a herbal tonic, that has helped the country subdue Covid-19 and stamp its authority over a global pandemic that has made nonsense of the muscles of France, US, Italy, Spain, UK, and Iran put together. Despite normalcy returning to the island country and school children resuming studies following a first of its kind plant-based tonic that's proven effective both in preventive and curative, WHO says a cure from an African address cannot be trusted.

The herbal medicine developed by the country's Malagasy Institute of Applied Research (MIAR) contains Artemisia – a plant cultivated on the island and used in the fight against malaria.

Madagascar has a landmass of approximately 587,041sqkm and a population of around 27 million. It reported its index cases on March 23 with 9 confirmed patients and by April 19th had a total of 121 cases, 59 recoveries, and no deaths, as of April 24th. It has been 5 days now and no new cases have been recorded in the country. Yet, WHO is still not convinced. Their only contention is that the vaccine is locally made. The argument is no longer whether it produces results. But what exactly is Madagascar doing differently?

- Testing and contact tracing is devoid of politics.
- School children receive compulsorily small doses of the tonic throughout the day, as they prepare to return to school.
- The plant-based tonic is also being distributed free to the most vulnerable in the country and sold at very low prices to others.
- Wealthy and financially strong Madagascans, politicians, and legislators purchase the tonic and make donations as their contribution towards funding more research.
- BBC reports scores of locals trooping out to receive the tonic as no lockdown is in place.
- The country has not welcomed any "outside" assistance.
- Their laboratory scientists, medicinal professors, consultants and doctors converged in labs working

their socks off, while their counterparts in the rest of Africa were dressed in 3-piece suits, tuxedos, and pyjamas, drinking choice wines, turning on swivel chairs, watching TV and ordering as few tests as possible.

- Scientists in the country presented their findings to their President who happily went on national TV and took doses of the syrup, which was then processed, made, and bottled.
- All proceeds from sales of the medicine are to be pushed back into their science research institutes.

Make no mistake! As long as a Covid-19 vaccine is not found in the so-called 'saner climes', the WHO may well not okay it! Take it or leave it. I am not a scientist, but whatever is in those Madagascan bottles, even if it cures a million people a day, won't make sense to WHO because it relates to Carbonites who are often treated like lepers. It is simple. A no brainer if you asked me.

What would you say?

As usual, the WHO want the patent, franchise, and proprietary to be domiciled in a Western address – America, UK, Canada, Norway and even Latin America. Name them. Don't be deceived! Those guys had already written us off long ago. With over 2000 people dropping dead daily in the US alone, Melinda Gates could only see dead bodies lining the streets of Africa. It is foolishness. But that mentality is not new!

Ok, why are African heads still yet to rally round Madagascar and give this therapy a global shot? Tell me! The World Health Organization has been accused of complicity in the handling of the pandemic. Even the President of the United States sent a letter about his disappointment.

Here is the letter:

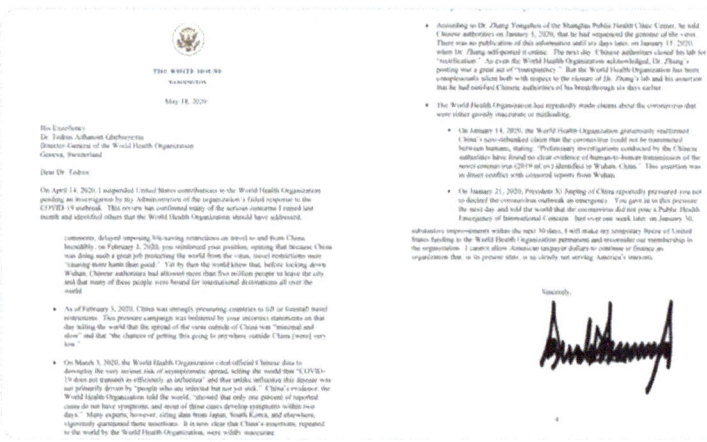

Donald J. Trump
@realDonaldTrump

This is the letter sent to Dr. Tedros of the World Health Organization. It is self-explanatory!

Credit: NPR.
https://www.npr.org/sections/goatsandsoda/2020/05/20/858911395/fact-checking-and-assessing-trumps-letter-of-rebuke-to-who

Though some people have rebuked the president's stance there is no denying that this virus wasn't appropriately managed. That is why it has spread around the world killing hundreds of thousands of people in a couple of months. The West sure have an agenda, but that agenda can't work without our culpable consent! Africa, please it's time to arise! We fought and won the war against the dreaded Ebola. The WHO did not give us any credits, but we didn't mind! We will win again, even against Covid-19. Collectively and in unity.

CHAPTER 7

THE CDC

Please check out the next article, it is quite long but it contains must-read information:

> *"Believe it or not, a coronavirus strain is patented by the Pirbright Institute, which is partially funded by the Bill and Melinda Gates Foundation. Another strain, which was isolated from humans, is owned by the CDC.*
>
> *The patent page for coronavirus explains that it "may be used as a vaccine for treating and/or preventing a disease, such as infectious bronchitis, in a subject," suggesting that this is just another weaponized viral strain designed to sell more useless, deadly vaccines, while at the same time killing off a few thousand, or perhaps a few million people.*

A close look at the patent page also shows that the
Pirbright Institute owns all sorts of other virus
patents, including one for African swine fever virus,
which is listed as a "vaccine."

It is thus no surprise that Bill Gates is a Pirbright
Institute financial backer, seeing as he's one of the
most aggressive, vaccine-pushing 'philanthropists' on
the planet.

(19) **United States**

(12) **Patent Application Publication** (10) Pub. No.: US 2017/0216427 A1
Bickerton et al. (43) Pub. Date: **Aug. 3, 2017**

(54) CORONAVIRUS

(71) Applicant: **THE PIRBRIGHT INSTITUTE**,
Pirbright, Woking (GB)

(72) Inventors: **Erica Bickerton**, Pirbright, Woking
(GB); **Sarah Keep**, Pirbright, Woking
(GB); **Paul Britton**, Pirbright, Woking
(GB)

(21) Appl. No.: 15/328,179

(22) PCT Filed: Jul. 23, 2015

(86) PCT No.: PCT/GB2015/052124
§ 371 (c)(1),
(2) Date: Jan. 23, 2017

(30) **Foreign Application Priority Data**

Jul. 23, 2014 (GB) 1413020.7

Publication Classification

(51) Int. Cl.
A61K 39/215 (2006.01)
C12N 9/12 (2006.01)
C12N 7/00 (2006.01)

(52) U.S. Cl.
CPC *A61K 39/215* (2013.01); *C12N 7/00*
(2013.01); *C12N 9/127* (2013.01); *C12Y*
207/07048 (2013.01); *C12N 2770/20021*
(2013.01); *C12N 2770/20022* (2013.01); *C12N*
2770/20034 (2013.01); *C12N 2770/20062*
(2013.01); *A61K 2039/5254* (2013.01)

(57) **ABSTRACT**

The present invention provides a live, attenuated coronavirus comprising a variant replicase gene encoding polypeptide(s) comprising a mutation in one or more of non-structural protein(s) (nsp)-10, nsp-14, nsp-15 or nsp-16. The coronavirus may be used as a vaccine for treating and/or preventing a disease, such as infectious bronchitis, in a subject.

And here is another patent for coronavirus, isolated from humans — Patent US7220852B1 – CORONAVIRUS a.k.a. SARS. The patent was granted to the CDC and the "inventors" are all American:

Patent US7220852B1 – CORONAVIRUS a.k.a. SARS

You can download the above patent HERE [.pdf].

The way this whole coronavirus situation is taking shape would seem to be exactly what Gates once proposed as a "solution" to the alleged problem of "overpopulation."

At an infamous TED Talk, Gates explained that vaccines are one of the keys to reducing global population levels, and what better way to do that than to unleash patented coronavirus on the masses in order to later introduce a patented vaccine for it?

Bill and Melinda Gates hosted "Event 201" back in October, described as a "high-level pandemic exercise"

What's further interesting is that the Bill and Melinda Gates Foundation co-hosted a "high-level pandemic exercise" back in October that involved discussions about how "public/private partnerships will be necessary during the response to a severe pandemic in order to diminish large-scale economic and societal consequences."

Held in partnership with the Johns Hopkins Center for Health Security and the World Economic Forum, this latest endeavor by Bill Gates is highly suspicious, to say the least, especially when considering that it was held just in time for the coronavirus outbreak.

As is usually the case with suspicious disease outbreaks that get the media and academia talking about new vaccines and public-private partnerships, **Bill Gates' fingerprints are almost always hiding in the background.**

And this is exactly the case with coronaviruses, which could accomplish many of Gates' expectations for the future, including mass depopulation, mass *vaccination and mass consolidation of government power.*

"These events are increasing, and they are disruptive to health, economies, and society," reads an announcement about "Event 201," as they called it, or the meeting with Gates and his cronies from back in October.

"Managing these events already strains global capacity, even absent a pandemic threat. Experts agree that it is only a matter of time before one of these pandemics becomes global – a pandemic with potentially catastrophic consequences. A severe pandemic, which becomes 'Event 201,' would require reliable cooperation among several industries, national governments, and key international institutions."

127

This reads like a predictive script for what we're now seeing with coronavirus, as governments around the world scramble to "manage" this deadly outbreak with martial law, vaccine fast-tracking, quarantines and plenty of fear-mongering.

"If we do a really great job on vaccines, health care, reproductive health services, we could lower [the global population] by perhaps about 10 to 15 percent," *Gates is infamously quoted as saying about the true intent of his "humanitarian" efforts.*

By Ethan Huff, Guest writer January 29, 2020 45

He added: "We still don't know precisely when COVID-19 was first introduced or how many people were infected. The only way we would have been able to know this is if we had been testing more broadly."

"The new CDC analysis was based on four lines of evidence, including an analysis of genetic sequences of the coronavirus, testing of specimens collected as part of routine monitoring for the flu, emergency room records and the cases of two people in California later discovered to have died from COVID-19 in early and mid-February."

Gerry Brooks complained about the directive given to schools on his Facebook: https://m.facebook.com/story.php?story_fbid=137730 52291457344&id=407074846168782

Gerry said that it is not possible to follow the CDC guidelines and put all desks 6ft apart as classes have between 20 to 50 kids. Not only this, but classrooms are just not big enough for this. The CDC is also proposing partitions in schools and just like Gerry

---

45 https://humansarefree.com/2020/01/bill-gates-pirbright-institute-cdc-patent-coronavirus.html?fbclid=IwAR3niSfPOY_axt4FqufiuDMA4A 1Iz2I1PBmk8EVMY5nvoCAsO6zDWY8rj4o accessed April 2nd 2020 @03:56

couldn't even address it, I too don't understand how that will work.

Another insane directive is that students cannot share toys or devices. How will finances be provided for individual toys, computers, and learning resources for every school child? It's impossible.

They also said there is to be no mixing of groups and classrooms in schools. So, teachers should stay in one classroom and all day long. Really?

There are many other directives they brought up which are insane and impossible.

https://mobile.facebook.com/story.php?story_fbid=13773 05229145734&id=407074846168782&_rdc=1&_rdr

According to https://arstechnica.com/science/2020/04
/cdcs-failed-coronavirus-tests-were-tainted-with-
coronavirus-feds-confirm/?fbclid=IwAR1xLHQb
MRNTFv5641CNaNsQIENCGsBMv8vG1nj-
Y9aNvhlEOIWW7sx8TFI, a federal investigation found
CDC researchers not following protocol. The CDC sent
states tainted testing kits in February that were
themselves seeded with the virus; federal officials
have confirmed. The contamination made the tests
uninterpretable, and—because testing is crucial for
containment efforts—it lost the country invaluable
time to get ahead of the advancing pandemic the
arstechnica website stated.

This is just tragic as more than 700 hundred thousand
confirmed coronavirus cases and over a hundred
thousand deaths have occurred. The CDC must be
brought to book over negligence. This is why the
President of the United States side-lined the public
health body.

Robert Redfield a director in the CDC has to concede
that the pandemic overwhelmed the CDC and there
might likely be a second wave of the pandemic later in
the year. This is sad news if you think of the havoc
that this pandemic has already caused. Though the
side-lining of the CDC has left the Trump-led
government with no concrete plan of managing this
pandemic, it seems Trump now has advisers who will
always inform him of the next course of action.

But it is no secret that the CDC has not managed this crisis well especially with test. The testing kits proved to be faulty with the problem compounded by sluggish efforts to rectify the deficiencies and then by severe bottlenecks in distributing enough tests to the public. How the CDC, which is one of the most respected public health agencies in the world, is now barely visible in the middle of a pandemic is something interesting to say the very least.

Let's move on.

Kwadw(o) Naya: Baa Ankh Em Ra A'lyun Eil

132

CHAPTER 8

FACT OR FICTION?

What is this?

A natural phenomenon? Pandemic? Epidemic? Scamdemic? Purging? Depopulation? Mass Torture and Genocide? Biowarfare? Or a mixture? Was it natural or deliberate? How did it come about? It all started in Wuhan in China, right?

Let us take a look, see if we can see what is going on, please have patience, this chapter may be very long as we have quite a lot to get through.

First let us check out the summary of events as detailed on the WHO's website:

"*Summary*

- *A pneumonia of unknown cause detected in Wuhan, China was first reported to the WHO Country Office in China on 31 December 2019.*

- *WHO is working 24/7 to analyse data, provide advice, coordinate with partners, help countries prepare, increase supplies and manage expert networks.*

- *The outbreak was declared a Public Health Emergency of International Concern on 30 January 2020.*

- *The international community has asked for US$675 million to help protect states with weaker health systems as part of its Strategic Preparedness and Response Plan.*

- *On 11 February 2020, WHO announced a name for the new coronavirus disease: COVID-19.*"[46]

On March 11th 2020 the director-general of WHO, Tedros Adhanom Ghebreyesus, or Tedros as he is known declared **COVID-19** a **pandemic. In their own words –** "*The worldwide spread of a new disease.*"

134

---

46 https://www.who.int/emergencies/diseases/novel-coronavirus-2019/events-as-they-happen accessed April 12th 2020 @22:23

So Tedros declared a global pandemic as we have seen, and our liberties have been taken away. We have been on lockdown for around 3 weeks in the UK. China has recently eased the lockdown after 80 days. Imagine that, it's like being on house arrest all in the name of good.

Coronavirus is not new. But which particular strain of the virus is COVID-19? Does anyone know? Is there really a novel coronavirus called COVID-19 or is that just a code name for something like Covert Virus – Identity Destruction Project-19 (or something like this?). And why the 19? Is it to represent 2019 or is it the symbolic 19 (Alpha and Omega?).

Did you know that there are several different strains of coronavirus that are floating around at the moment? I must admit it is very confusing, but I guess that was the idea, the plan. For example, when the virus first hit China only Chinese people appeared to be getting affected by it. It also reportedly spread to another 53 countries quite quickly but then again it was the same result, it seemed to be that only Chinese people were getting coronavirus. Could this be some biological warfare?

It is common knowledge that China has been having trade wars with the US. It is also common knowledge that China won the 5G race, did you see all that confusion with Huwaei? I do not want to look at this from a conspiracy theorist perspective, but I wouldn't want us to miss any facts. Please check out the next extract from an article by Peter Koenig, a global researcher. I would advise you to read the full article when you get the chance, there he gives his full insight into the COVID-19 situation:

> *"Also, at this time it becomes increasingly important to remind people that the outbreak in China was targeting the Chinese genome. Did it later mutate to transgress the 'borders' of Chinese DNA? When did that happen, if it happened? Because at the beginning it was clear that even the infected victims in other parts of the world, were to 99.9% of Chinese descent.*
>
> *What happened later, when the virus spread to Italy and Iran, is another issue, and opens the way to a number of speculations.*
>
> *(i) There were various strains of the virus circulated in sequence – so as to destabilize countries around the world and to confound the populace and media, so that especially nobody of the mainstream may come to the conclusion that the first strain was targeting China in a bio-war.*
>
> *(ii) In Iran, I have a strong suspicion that the virus was an enhanced form of MERS (Middle East Respiratory Syndrome, man-made, broke out first in Saudi Arabia in 2012, directed to the Arabic genome) – which was somehow introduced into government circles (by aerosol spray?) – with the goal of "Regime Change" by COVID19-caused death. Its Washington's wishful thinking for at least the last 30 years.*

(iii) In Italy – why Italy? – Maybe because Washington / Brussels wanted to hit Italy hard for having been officially the first country to sign a Belt and Road (BRI) accord with China (actually the first was Greece, but nobody is supposed to know that China came to the rescue of Greece, destroyed by Greece's brothers, the EU members, mainly Germany and France).

(iv) The hype about the high death to infection rate in Italy, as of the time of this writing: 10,149 infections vs. 631 deaths = death rate of 6.2 (comparatively Iran: 8042 infections vs. 291 deaths = 3.6 death rate). The death rate of Italy is almost double that of Iran and almost ten-fold that of average Europe. (Are these discrepancies the result of failures in the establishing reliable data pertaining to "infections", see our observations pertaining to Italy below).

Why? – Was is Italy being affected with virus panic? Was there a much stronger strain introduced to Italy?

The common flu in Europe in the 2019 / 2020 season, has apparently so far killed about 16,000 (in the US the death toll is, according to CDC between 14,000 and 32,000, depending on which CDC website you look at).

> *Could it be that among the Italian coronavirus deaths there were also common flu victims, as the affected victims are mostly elderly with respiratory preconditions? Also, symptoms are very similar between coronavirus and the common flu, and nobody questions and checks the official authorities' narrative?"* [47]

When looking into these anomalies it always seems that we find more questions than answers. Firstly, on what pretext, basis or evidence did Tedros have to make this big call? To prompt him to declare a global pandemic? And is this (so-called) pandemic real or orchestrated?

Let us take a look:

1) On what basis or evidence did Tedros have to make this big call?

Under the advice of Faucci, Dr Neil Ferguson and Bill Gates.

Please read the next extract:

---

47 https://www.lewrockwell.com/2020/03/no_author/the-coronavirus-covid-19-pandemic-the-real-danger-is-agenda-id2020/ accessed April 13th @19:24

"

The Common Roots of...

'Climate Change and COVID-19 Hysteria'

by Patrick Wood March 29, 2020 from TechnocracyNews

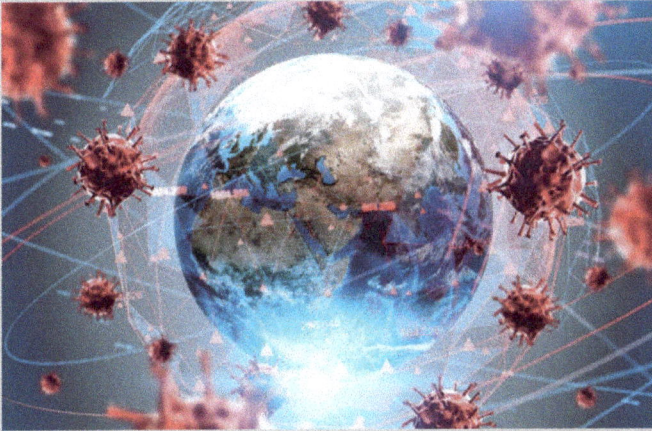

Licensed through Adobe Stock

"Introduction

People want to know just how bad is the COVID-19 virus and is fighting it worth the destruction of the world's economic and financial system while disrupting the lives of hundreds of millions of people?

The story behind the story will make it clear that things are seldom as they seem. In short and when seen through the lens of Sustainable Development, aka Technocracy, the whole world has just been punked and then panicked into destroying itself over COVID-19.

The culprit...?

A world-class Technocrat in Britain:

Dr. **Neil Ferguson**, PhD is a professor at Imperial College in London that bills itself as a "global university". It is thoroughly steeped in Sustainable Development and more dedicated to social causes than academic achievement.

In fact, Imperial is very well-known for its alarmist research reports on climate change, carbon reduction, environmental degradation, loss of biodiversity, etc.

The problem with the <u>global warming meme</u> is that it is a tired, worn-out racehorse that much of the world simply ignores.

Global warming alarmists have tried every trick in the book to stampede the world into Sustainable Development. They have knowingly falsified climate data, flooded the world with inaccurate academic reports, held world meetings like the Paris Accord in France, threatened and bullied their critics, created a global youth movement to shame leaders into action, etc.

All of these strategies have failed to usher in the UN's 'Sustainable Development,' aka 'Technocracy,' and show little promise of success in the future.

What the Sustainable Development crowd needed was to put their non-performing racehorse "Global Warming" out to pasture and find a brand new horse that could finally run and win the race to what the UN calls "deep transformation" of the entire global economic system.

The new horse is named "COVID-19".

Different horse, same jockey, same race, same finish line..."

"The Work Begins

*Once the release of COVID-19 in Wuhan was recognized as a potential pandemic, academic researcher Dr. **Neil Ferguson** went to work developing a computer model to track and forecast its rapid spread.*

At the top of his field, Ferguson is a professor of mathematical biology at Imperial College in London, and has had extensive experience in tracking other infectious diseases such as the,

- <u>Swine Flu in 2009</u>

- <u>Dengue in 2015</u>

- <u>Zika in 2016</u>...

Ferguson is a British epidemiologist and a professor of mathematical biology at Imperial College. According to the World Health Organization (WHO),

Epidemiology is the study of the distribution and determinants of health-related states or events (including disease), and the application of this study to the control of diseases and other health problems. Various methods can be used to carry out epidemiological investigations: surveillance and descriptive studies can be used to study distribution; analytical studies are used to study determinants.

With a Master of Arts degree in physics, he received a Doctor of Philosophy degree in theoretical physics. He has no medical or related degree, but rather chose to apply his education to use his mathematical skills by modeling the spread of infectious diseases.

In other words, Ferguson is a data-driven Technocrat with direct access to policy-makers around the world. According to the New York Times,

Imperial College has advised the government on its response to previous epidemics, including SARS, avian flu and swine flu.

With ties to the World Health Organization and a team of 50 scientists, led by a prominent epidemiologist, Neil Ferguson, Imperial is treated as a sort of gold standard, its mathematical models feeding directly into government policies.

Ferguson's COVID-19 Study

Early on in the COVID-19 outbreak, Ferguson began to advise officials in Britain and the United States on the spread of the infection as well as ways to fight it.

Thus, he served as both researcher and policy advisor at the same time.

Ferguson's conclusion that COVID-19 would kill as many as 500,000 people in Britain and over 1.1 million in the United States, set off a tidal wave of panic that has not subsided.

His policy recommendations were just as shocking, namely, that societies must be entirely locked down in order to survive.

On March 16, 2020, Ferguson finally released his formal report, <u>Impact of Non-Pharmaceutical Interventions (NPIs) to reduce COVID19 Mortality and Healthcare Demand</u>.

Here are some quick observations from reading this report:

- *Well before publishing, he advised policy makers. His modeling study "informed policymaking in the UK and other countries in recent weeks"*

- *Comparable to 1918 Spanish flu: "it represents the most serious seen in a respiratory virus since the 1918 H1N1 influenza pandemic"*

- *Applied this and previous model to UK and US: "we apply a previously published microsimulation model to two countries: the UK (Great Britain specifically) and the US"*

- *There are two possible strategies: Mitigation and Suppression*

- *Mitigation: This proposed social distancing, home-isolation of sick, home-quarantine of relatives, "We find that optimal mitigation policies (combining home isolation of suspect cases, home quarantine of those living in the same household as suspect cases, and social distancing of the elderly and others at most risk of severe disease) might reduce peak healthcare demand by 2/3 and deaths by half"*

- *In spite of reducing deaths by half, "the resulting mitigated epidemic would still likely result in hundreds of thousands of deaths and health systems (most notably intensive care units) being overwhelmed many times over"*

144

- *Thus, he argues that Suppression is the only option*

- *Suppression: Additional measures include social distancing of the entire population, home isolation of infected, household quarantine of family members, school and university closures*

- *Long term: Suppression "will need to be maintained until a vaccine becomes available (potentially 18 months or more)".*

These doomsday predictions, based entirely on computer simulations similar to those used in climate studies, were believable enough that national leaders accepted them at face value.

Worse, they also accepted Ferguson's policy recommendations, which were then implemented with precise detail. Here are some of the more prescient excerpts from the report's conclusion section:

Our results demonstrate that it will be necessary to layer multiple interventions, regardless of whether suppression or mitigation is the overarching policy goal.

However, suppression will require the layering of more intensive and socially disruptive measures than mitigation.

The choice of interventions ultimately depends on the relative feasibility of their implementation and their likely effectiveness in different social contexts.

(p. 14)

Overall, our results suggest that population-wide social distancing applied to the population as a whole would have the largest impact; and in combination with other interventions - notably home isolation of cases and school and university closure - has the potential to suppress transmission below the threshold of R=1 required to rapidly reduce case incidence.

A minimum policy for effective suppression is therefore population-wide social distancing combined with home isolation of cases and school and university closure.

To avoid a rebound in transmission, these policies will need to be maintained until large stocks of vaccine are available to immunize the population - which could be 18 months or more.

Technology - such as mobile phone apps that track an individual's interactions with other people in society - might allow such a policy to be more effective and scalable if the associated privacy concerns can be overcome.

(p.15)

Perhaps our most significant conclusion is that mitigation is unlikely to be feasible without emergency surge capacity limits of the UK and US healthcare systems being exceeded many times over.

In the most effective mitigation strategy examined, which leads to a single, relatively short epidemic (case isolation, household quarantine and social distancing of the elderly), the surge limits for both general ward and ICU beds would be exceeded by at least 8-fold under the more optimistic scenario for critical care requirements that we examined.

In addition, even if all patients were able to be treated, we predict there would still be in the order of 250,000 deaths in GB, and 1.1-1.2 million in the US.

(p. 16)

The **mind of a Technocrat** *can be clearly seen in this whole package.*

All of these draconian measures must be maintained until a **vaccine** *is created, which is at least 18 months. The use of mobile phone apps to track the world's population could be effective if citizens could be railroaded into it.*

What is not seen is one word about the destruction of the global economic system that would certainly result from these draconian policy measures.

> *Climate alarmists who articulated <u>the Green New</u> <u>Deal</u> policies also call for radical measures to transform society and they are likewise silent about the inevitable destructive effects such policies would have on the global economy."*[48]

You can read the full article at the footnote below.

As you can see, many thanks to Dr Ferguson and the imperial college, the whole world has been driven to believe in this **COVID-19 SCAMDEMIC.** Preempting our leaders to implement draconian measures across the globe. Funnily enough, Dr Ferguson has just resigned from his post due to breaking social distancing regulations, even though Dr Ferguson earlier stated that 250,000 people could die without drastic action. Despite this, he allowed a woman he was said to be in a relationship to visit his home. This is not the half of it really.

Dr Anthony Faucci has also been getting his hands dirty for many, many years through the reign of several presidents. He was heavily involved in the **HIV** and AIDS **SCAMDEMICS.** Dr Faucci is an American physician and immunologist who has served as the director of the National Institute of Allergy and Infectious Diseases since 1984. Since January 2020, he

---

48 https://www.bibliotecapleyades.net/ciencia3/ciencia_
climatechange175.htm accessed April 16th 2020 @08:19

has been one of the lead members of the Trump Administration's White House Coronavirus Task Force addressing the 2019–20 coronavirus pandemic in the United States. He is the one in charge of the US response to the Coronavirus Epidemic. Of course, Dr Fauci has his occult followers just like other people who are out to deceive the world.

IN FAUCI WE TRUST

OLIVE BRANCH BAR + RESTAURANT
NEWBRUNSWICKTAKEOUT.COM

TEEFILM.COM

He has proven to be inconsistent in his video. Watch his interview here:
https://www.youtube.com/watch?v=zGamIC504po

Did you know that the US has sent around 3.7 million dollars (if not more) to a laboratory in Wuhan to have them to research coronavirus in bats? Fauci's NIAID were the ones who funded this research project.

Dr Anthony Fauci, the head of the National Institute For Health, is the same Fauci who reportedly commissioned the 3.7 million dollar Wuhan research.

Isn't this a bit of a contradiction?

The same guy who is funding the creation of viruses and vaccines is the same one who is spearheading the campaign to control the outbreak. Does this even make sense?

It is common knowledge that George Soros has a factory in Wuhan that deals with virology. It is also common knowledge that the Bill and Sheila Gates and the Clinton Foundations have heavily invested millions upon millions in the testing and creation of vaccines as well as strategies for controlling outbreaks, epidemics and pandemics. We only have to look at event 201 to know.

Sometimes things are done nicely and quietly but in our faces. Many of us have been channelled so much information from our tel.**lie**.visions that we are now programmed Autobots that can be programmed on demand. That is not to mention Johnson and Johnson's involvement. If the government told us that we would be locked down for life as the virus will be around forever, most would do so without question. Or if they said that the cure was to run around the block naked 3 times after you have applied some vaseline to your bottom, many would follow the instructions or the recommended guidelines without question.

Am I lying?

Check out the next extracts please:

Additionally, the *Daily Mail* reported that National Institutes of Healt which Fauci's NIAID is a member, provided a $3.7 million grant to th Wuhan Institute of Virology to study bat-borne coronavirus.

That study was headlined, 'Discovery of a rich gene pool of bat SARS related coronaviruses provides new insights into the origin of SARS coronavirus.'

Around the Web

Here's an excerpt from the April 4, 2018 NIAID website entry entitled "New Coronavirus Emerges From Bats in China, Devastates Young Swine": "A newly identified coronavirus that killed nearly 25,000 piglets in 2016-17 in China emerged from horseshoe bats near the origin of the severe acute respiratory syndrome coronavirus (SARS-CoV), which emerged in 2002 in the same bat species. The new virus is named swine acute diarrhea syndrome coronavirus (SADS-CoV). It does not appear to infect people, unlike SARS-CoV which infected more than 8,000 people and killed 774. No SARS-CoV cases have been identified since 2004. The study investigators identified SADS-CoV on four pig farms in China's Guangdong Province. The work was a collaboration among scientists from EcoHealth Alliance, Duke-NUS Medical School, Wuhan Institute of Virology and other organizations, and was funded by the National Institute of Allergy and Infectious Diseases, part of the National Institutes of Health. The research is published in the journal *Nature*. The researchers say the finding is an important reminder that identifying new viruses in animals and quickly determining their potential to infect people is a key way to reduce global

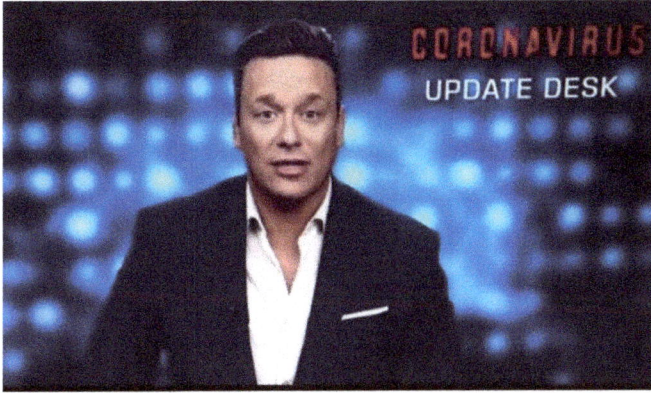

Dr. Anthony Fauci's National Institute of Allergy and Infectious Diseases (NIAID) actually funded a study on Bat Coronavirus, which was a project that included scientists at the Wuhan Institute of Virology, the Chinese lab at the center of controversy over their bat research. That study confirmed in 2018 that humans have died from coronavirus.

(RELATED: Read The FULL STORY of FAUCI and BILL GATES).

REVEALED: U.S. government gave $3.7million grant to Wuhan lab at center of coronavirus leak scrutiny that was performing experiments on bats from the caves where the disease is believed to have originated

- The US National Institutes of Health, a government agency, awarded a $3.7million research grant to the Wuhan Institute of Virology
- The lab is the center of several conspiracy theories that suggest it is the original source of the coronavirus outbreak
- The institute experimented on bats from the source of the coronavirus
- They were captured more than 1,000 miles away in Yunnan
- Sequencing of the Covid-19 genome has traced it to bats to Yunnan's caves
- The U.S. government funded research on coronavirus transmission in the lab over the past decade
- Learn more about how to help people impacted by COVID

The Chinese laboratory at the center of scrutiny over a potential coronavirus leak has been using U.S. government money to carry out research on bats from the caves which scientists believe are the original source of the deadly outbreak.

The Wuhan Institute of Virology undertook coronavirus experiments on mammals captured more than 1,000 miles away in Yunnan which were funded by a $3.7 million grant from the US government.

Sequencing of the COVID-19 genome has traced it back to bats found in Yunnan caves but it was first thought to have transferred to humans at an animal market in Wuhan.

The revelation that the Wuhan Institute was experimenting on bats from the area already known to be the source of COVID-19 - and doing so with American money - has sparked further fears that the lab, and not the market, is the original outbreak source.

When is this going to stop?

When are we going to start critically thinking?

When are we going to start analyzing the root of our problems and situations, looking at who the benefactors are each time?

It always tells us a lot knowing who is going to be gaining from each situation, realizing and recognising ulterior motives if there is any. Many of us do not do this. For the world to change we need to first.

2) **Is this (so-called) pandemic real or orchestrated?**

Before we go into this, let me reiterate the questions we have been asking all day long.

https://www.facebook.com/ScienceNaturePage/videos/196253568151309/

According to this must-watch video, it's been discovered that a publication was already published postulating the coming of this pandemic. Why did nobody do anything about it?

I have my thoughts regarding this but I feel that we should look at some more factors in the equation before making a decision. Please check out the following extract. It is from an undisclosed source but the author does a good job in putting a few facts together. There is a lot more to this story but this is a very good start:

BACKGROUND AND KEY INFO RE CORONAVIRUS AND THE AGENDA BEHIND IT

April 13, 2020

THE FOLLOWING IS A LIST OF SUBSTANTIATED
FACTS ABOUT CV SENT TO ME BY A CONTACT.
BELOW THAT ARE MY COMMENTS AND MORE INFO.

We know the following. Here are the facts:

1. George Soros owns WuXi Pharma Biotech
    Laboratory, located at 666 Gaoxin Rd., East Lake
    High Tech Development Zone, Wuhan, 430075
    China. (Yes, you got that street address correct.)

2. Through financial disclosures we know he has
    invested at least 100 million dollars in
    establishing this company/facility. It will be
    manufacturing the vaccine for profit. Bill Gates
    probably owns a piece of it.

3. The US military and China were investigating
    bat virus jointly. In 2014 the US pulled out and
    withdrew all funding, saying that what they
    were doing was too dangerous and risky. The
    Chinese government then assumed full
    support. That is when George Soros decided to
    pay for and build this lab.

4. We know that world-class scientists from
    Europe and the USA have worked at this lab —
    often secretly. A Harvard professor has recently
    been arrested by the FBI for spying. He failed to
    disclose that he had secretly been working at
    this lab, and under his defense contract he was
    supposed to.

5.   *The cabal owns and controls NATO. Many think the virus was released by a NATO commando group at the World Military Games in Wuhan. Three years ago a secret induced pandemic plan was circulated (and leaked) among the top brass at NATO Headquarters in Geneva.*

The Military Games is basically a remake of the Olympics, but the difference is, paid professional athletes in military organizations are allowed to compete. There were 9,308 athletes competing from 109 countries. If you wanted to jumpstart a worldwide pandemic, how could you find a better opportunity? The Stadium was only a few miles from the Soros Big Pharma Lab. The lab was also only a few miles from the fish market.

The Chinese themselves, and many others, have concluded the corona-19 pandemic was started at the Wuhan Military Games, at or near the closing ceremonies, in October 2019. From there, through the athletes, it rapidly spread around the world. The Chinese garment workers who did all the fabulous costumes and uniforms for the opening and closing ceremonies, returned to the fashion district in Italy, where they live, and took the virus with them.

6.   *There were several head fakes. The pandemic was started in a way that makes the Chinese suspicious of the Americans and the Americans suspicious of the Chinese. It was not started by either, it was started by Soros, NATO and the*

157

"deep state". The "deep state" would love to get a war going between China and the USA.

7.   OK. What is, who is, the "deep state"? You need to know the answer to this question to understand what happened in Wuhan China. In a sentence, the "deep state" is a network of people in and out of government, especially in the CIA, FBI, DOJ, US Military, Congress, and the US State Department who are loyal to, and looking out for the interests of the people who own the big Jewish banks and their international financial system. But it is bigger than just the US. They have people placed in many other governments around the world as well. These people own the Big Banks, Big Oil, Big Pharma, Big Ag, and most of the media and news organizations, including Reuters and AP. Their corporations are huge and international. They own every national bank in every country around the world except for three — they own the FED in the USA. For instance, there are a whole bunch of people in the CIA who are openly doing secret operations, gathering information and feeding that information to the big banks. Some of what they do is illegal and clandestine, but nobody stops them. Some people in the CIA and FBI are spying on the Big Bank's enemies. In the same way, some well placed people in the FDA, and WHO, and other

> *health organizations have subverted their agencies to look out for Big Pharma.*

The first thing we need to understand, is the Soros Wuhan bio lab virus was made to serve the interests of Big Pharma. It is evil. It is intended to eventually reduce the world population, because that is what the cabal wants, but they want to do it in a way where "they" make money off of the people who are dying. This is how they think. They want to manage the people who get sick, and who eventually die. They don't want to kill them quickly, like in a mass pandemic, until they have gotten every penny they can out of it. The Soros-Wuhan lab created the virus and it has already developed a vaccine. Both are a scam. The vaccine will be just as evil as the virus, maybe worse. What they end up putting into people will be different than what they are currently testing. Don't expect their "vaccine" to heal people. It is going to make things worse. Neither China nor the USA wants a pandemic or a war. Only the Banksters do. — an undisclosed source[49]

---

[49] http://projectcamelotportal.com/2020/04/13/background-and-key-info-re-coronavirus/?fbclid=IwAR1GXkXEktkotFTbBBS8EosfrM1lPMb_XQqQqLJjFRPx-IpmnBkhTc7xbUk accessed April 13th 2020 @22:58

So, is this (so-called) pandemic real or orchestrated?

1) Considering everything that we have looked at in this book today so far, we haven't really seen any signs of this being a pandemic at all, have we? I feel that we can only say that this has been orchestrated unless the patents for the virus are fake. Why would anyone want to make or manufacture a virus? That is not even mentioning the predictive programming or the prior virus test simulations which Bill Gates and co have been involved with.

   What would you say?

   It looks very orchestrated, deliberate, (with an end goal in mind) but we know that there is major corruption throughout the globe and blackmail, that usually boils down to the misuse of money, power or sex.

   You see a pandemic is a very big thing. I am not saying that COVID-19 is small but it is definitly not that. I will show you.

   But let us have a look at these images first:

ICU NURSE SPEAKS OUT ABOUT
COVID-19 IMPROPER DIAGNOSIS
etheriumblack 6 d
145 views • 4 comments
Up Next
13:28

Once they're RULED OUT, they don't say
'oh nevermind, scratch that number...'
the NUMBER STAYS!"

They're considered COvid
until it's ruled out

> You can say there are COvid patients being admitted for COvid, but

> We can't disclose this technically to ANYONE...or you are breaking FEDERAL LAW.

Covid-19 is no pandemic.

You see a **"pandemic"** is usually a condition, where the death to infection rate reaches more than 12%. At the time of the WHO's announcement, the death rate in Europe was approximately 0.4%. Italy was a special case, where the peak of the death rate was 6%.

So is this COVID-19 malarky a natural phenomenon?

HELL NO! The **FACTS** SPEAK OTHERWISE as WE can SEE!

Is it an EPIDEMIC or SCAMDEMIC?

Let us take a look at today's COVID-19 figures. It might help us get some perspective on this.

Let US SEE what is going on in China, the UK, and the US:

We will start with the US as it has the most confirmed cases in the world.

In the US, **2,973,208** people were tested (which is worrying, to say the least). From this, there has been **598,670** officially confirmed cases, **470,747** people who have recovered and **125,196** total deaths.

In the UK, there has been **94,845** officially confirmed cases with **12,129** total deaths.

In China, there has been **83,306** confirmed cases and **3,345** deaths.[50]

As of June 8, there are 7,037,059 cases of Covid-19 across the globe, with 4344 of them leading to death.

---

50 https://gisanddata.maps.arcgis.com/apps/opsdashboa rd/index.html#/bda7594740fd4029942346 7b48e9ecf6 accessed April 14th 2020 @23:13 (Last Updated at 4/14/2020, 8:20:58 PM)

I don't want to give percentages but it is plain to see what is going on. China seems to be dealing with the situation with most people recovering. In the US (as you can see), they have a large number of confirmed cases, more than anyone else in the world, 125,196 total deaths with 470,747 pulling through. But why are so many people dying?

On June 15, 38 people supposedly died from the COVID in the UK which made a total of 41,737 deaths. Also as from June 15, masks are compulsory on public transport and in public places. Social distancing still applies which is causing more and more queues. I don't know why masks are compulsory in public when so many leading experts have said masks will never stop the virus. Apparantly, masks do more damage than good as they sometimes lead to respiratory problems.

165

As I said before, if you are in the UK I feel sorry for you. I don't know what else to say regarding this but it probably explains the reason why I do not get involved with the NHS in any way shape or form, having a preference to natural, holistic methods.

If you catch coronavirus in the UK, you may as well arrange your own funeral.

I do not LIE.

FACTS don't either.

As I say credit where credit is due, China has done very well. They seem to have the virus under control.

What is going on?

This is not an EPIDEMIC, SCAMDEMIC, maybe, GENOCIDE and TORTURE for sure. Especially because viruses do not exist per se (I will get into that a little later). It may well be purging going on or depopulation.

It is hard to say anything at present... but purging? Depopulation? Mass Torture? Genocide? Or Biowarfare?

I would never leave these factors out.

Did you know that there is no such thing as a deadly virus? Not as we know it. Ask any skilled doctor or virologist, they will confirm this for you. We have viruses and we have Charlie and the Chocolate Factory – I will attempt to explain.

You SEE WE have a lot going on inside us. Inside the human body are millions of viruses and bacteria, just like cells and other organisms. If we are unlucky we might find the odd bug or two. These viruses and bacteria are normal and there for a purpose, usually protecting the body. They only tend to mass reproduce when something triggers it. Stress on our immune system, anxiety, bad food, drugs, alcohol, and so on. There's no such thing as pathogenic viruses (the ones we are often taught to fear, but there is such a thing as a virus). It is normal, natural, NATURE.

Please check out the next extract before I explain some more:

> *"Pesticide manufacturers, pharmaceutical giants, the U.S. government, industry scientists, the Centers for Disease Control (CDC), State and County government agencies believe in their own fairy tales. But they find those children's stories too boring and too happy. They wanted something dark and sinister. So they rewrote the fairytale and thought of some scary name that evokes fear of the unknown: "West Nile Virus". Then, rather than good people who give children presents and good feelings, this West Nile Virus is a mean and ugly monster. It kills people, it's contagious, and they want you to think that you should be very afraid of it. They want you to be so afraid of it that you will vote for your local governmental agency to go ahead and spray chemicals on you (and some mosquitoes) to stop it. But you know what? Just like the Easter Bunny and all the others, it just doesn't exist. Let me explain.*
>
> *"Dr. Koch's common sense postulates, which set up the criteria to prove the existence of a virus, used to be a part of science. As technology improved science should have been able to conclusively prove the existence of viruses under Koch's postulates and at least isolate and locate a virus under a microscope. But scientists never have been able to do this.*

167

> *Nobody could isolate any viruses to prove that they exist. Rather than admit that perhaps infectious viruses do not exist, dubious scientists now thought of a better plan. They decided to pretend viruses exist. To do that they had to claim the virus find fits into Koch's accepted postulates. So they write and use the term "isolated" for a virus even when they have done no such thing.*
>
> **The idea of a virus causing disease was purposely spread as a disinformation strategy and now everybody believes in it. " – Dr Rami Nagel**[51]

As you can SEE, true viruses are not as most of us know it. Many doctors have come out and confirmed this recently such as Dr Nagel, Dr Shiv, Dr Buttar, and Dr Judy Mikovits as well as many more. Around twenty highly skilled medical doctors and professionals have spoken out during this pandemic to give their WORD.

Dr Shiv has recently explained that COVID-19 was actually manufactured by the deep state to push 3 agendas:

1) To crash the economy
2) Suppress dissent
3) Push mandated vaccines and medicines

---

51 https://www.naturalnews.com/024754.html accessed April 30th 2020 @15:28

He explains how Dr Fauci and co. are involved in fake science and probably the biggest fraud that the world has ever seen. Making the world believe that the immune system is so weak that we always characterize some virus as the cause of destruction to the immune system. They also did this with HIV and AIDS. The goal is to scare everyone with a fake science understanding as though the immune system gets attacked by the virus.

Dr Shiv explains how doctors and nurses across the world are just realizing that they are now victims of a big pharma medical education system fraud. As the process is not focused on teaching people how to heal, it doesn't teach them to treat the body as a system, its not a process that teaches physicians how to use nutrition to heal the body. They just become automatons who just follow instructions. Most of these individuals have studied for many years, they go into careers with noble intentions to heal and save the world and make their families proud.

Many medical professionals are now waking up to this big pharma fraud. They are all speaking out because they are under Hippocratic Oath.

Let me explain the Hippocratic Oath:

Hippocratic Oath: One of the oldest binding documents in history, the Oath was written by Hippocrates is still held sacred by physicians: to treat the ill to the best of one's ability, to preserve a patient's privacy, to teach the secrets of medicine to the next generation, and so on.

A Modern Version of the Hippocratic Oath

I swear to fulfill, to the best of my ability and judgment, this covenant:

I will respect the hard-won scientific gains of those physicians in whose steps I walk, and gladly share such knowledge as is mine with those who are to follow.

I will apply, for the benefit of the sick, all measures which are required, avoiding those twin traps of overtreatment and therapeutic nihilism.

I will remember that there is an art to medicine as well as science, and that warmth, sympathy, and understanding may outweigh the surgeon's knife or the chemist's drug.

I will not be ashamed to say, "I know not," nor will I fail to call in my colleagues when the skills of another are needed for a patient's recovery.

I will respect the privacy of my patients, for their problems are not disclosed to me that the world may know. Most especially must I tread with care in matters of life and death. If it is given me to save a life, all thanks. But it may also be within my power to take a life; this awesome responsibility must be faced with great humbleness and awareness of my own frailty. Above all, I must not play at God.

I will remember that I do not treat a fever chart, a cancerous growth, but a sick human being, whose illness may affect the person's family and economic stability. My responsibility includes these related problems if I am to care adequately for the sick.

I will prevent disease whenever I can, for prevention is preferable to cure.

I will remember that I remain a member of society, with special obligations to all my fellow human beings, those sound of mind and body as well as the infirm.

If I do not violate this oath, may I enjoy life and art, respected while I live and remembered with affection thereafter. May I always act so as to preserve the finest traditions of my calling and may I long experience the joy of healing those who seek my help.

This oath places responsibility on lots of doctors to come and speak out.

Dr Sebi was saying the same thing as Dr Shiv. He used holistic electric foods to heal people from illnesses... we all seen what happened. And YOU still want to go and support big pharmaceuticals? Not me, sorry.

You can stay with Dr Fauci, stay with Bill Gates, the one who wants to push forced vaccination mandates but is unwilling to get himself or his family vaccinated? George Soros, the WHO and the CDC, Dr Ferguson, Johnson & Johnson, The Pirbrite Institute, Rockafellas, Rothschilds, The Bill and Melinda Gates Foundation, The Clinton Foundation, et al. REALLY?

I have heard many skilled doctors say the same about viruses, the fact that they do not exist, well not as THEY SAY.

I stumbled across this article:

> ### *"Dr Anthony Fauci: Globalist Snake Oil Salesman*
>
> *Here's confirmation Fauci has been working with Wellcome Trust & The Pirbright Institute (UK) (Coronavirus patent holder) for a long time.*
>
> *From Wikileaks archives:*
>
> *Moral: This 2009 C.I.A. propaganda document proves Coronavirus is not Fauci's first rodeo at fooling the public with fake pandemics to enrich his Big Pharma intelligence handlers*
>
> *Sean Noonan. (Sep. 21, 2009). US/FLU- Young children need 2 doses of H1N1 vaccine- US [incl. Anthony Fauci NIH]. Stratfor, Reuters, The Global Intelligence Files, Wikileaks Email-ID 1680879.*

https://wikileaks.org/gifiles/docs/16/1680879_us-flu-young-children-need-2-doses-of-h1n1-vaccine-us-.html

http://www.alertnet.org/thenews/newsdesk/N21313516.htm

Young children need 2 doses of H1N1 vaccine- US
21 Sep 2009 17:45:44 GMT
Source: Reuters
* Children 10 to 17 need one dose of swine flu vaccine

Dr. Anthony Fauci, director of the National Institute of Allergy and Infectious Diseases, said young children will likely need to have their doses 21 days apart. But he said they could receive seasonal flu shots and H1N1 shots on the same day -- something that could ease the logistics of vaccinating children multiple times.

About 25 companies globally are now making H1N1 vaccine.

The United States had ordered 195 million doses of H1N1 vaccine from five makers -- GlaxoSmithKline <GSK.L>, Sanofi, Australia's CSL <CSL.AX>, AstraZeneca's <AZN.L> MedImmune unit and Novartis <NOVN.AX>. With the new order from Sanofi, that would make more than 222 million doses.

https://wikileaks.org/gifiles/docs/16/1680879_us-flu-young-children-need-2-doses-of-h1n1-vaccine-us-.html

GlaxoSmithKline (the Wellcome Trust), Sanofi, AstraZeneca and Novartis are tightly aligned with the Bill and Melinda Gates Foundation, Merial Animal Heath Institute (UK & China), The Pirbright Institute funded by DARPA (U.S.) & DERA (UK)."[52]

---

52 https://truthbits.blog/2020/03/21/dr-fauci-globalist-snake-oil-salesman/ accessed April 16th 2020 @13:40

THE NANOTECHNOLOGY PLAN.

The plan now is to give us a never before Human approved RNA (synthetic DNA) vaccine along with a "Quantom Dot" track/trace nanotechnology implant connected to blockchain data on a global grid. (https://www.ledgerinsights.com/nanotechnology-blockchain-covid-19-immunity-passports/?fbclid=IwAR094gKBdtPRpgMbmfoVFw5cc mWHrI7ocGJu8CcEzXj4KN9_NT_fYKbG6sw)

https://www.sciencedirect.com/science/article/pii/B97 81845695880500127?fbclid=IwAR1Pzp1ByaGT07ojeSa7 NqNLZMY-CgKctYZPbhcMvK0KAAKfxpwGURM8ZWc

https://www.nature.com/articles/nnano.2015.115?fbcli d=IwAR2ykHqdHjsPPI1S9dcPLGsoi00Qy5k-owT1FxjkK61k_BVSMEnt7TW4qkY

https://www.ntno.org/v01p0244.htm?fbclid=IwAR11Hv zqGknAIeZbajfFhokFVWjU6ltjk_fsb32EBlje_II6I1f96C PJBtc

There are two ways of looking at things: the agents' way and the aware persons' way. The agent prescribes, adheres to, and defends profusely the profit-making scams of the rich and superwealthy controlling entities. The agents support these people whatever news is rolled out in the media and these very same rich and superwealthy are the first to not think about the agents (pawns) that defend and protect them, serve and idolize.

Let me give you eight more experts who are questioning the coronavirus pandemic:

1. **Dr John Lee** is an English consultant histopathologist at Rotherham General Hospital in South Yorkshire, England and formerly clinical professor of pathology at Hull York Medical School.

He is known to the wider public as the co-presenter (with Gunther von Hagens) of Anatomy for Beginners, *Autopsy: Life and Death* and *Autopsy: Emergency Room.*

This is what he says:

> *"But there's another, potentially even more serious problem: the way that deaths are recorded. If someone dies of a respiratory infection in the UK, the specific cause of the infection is not usually recorded, unless the illness is a rare 'notifiable disease."*

So the vast majority of respiratory deaths in the UK are recorded as bronchopneumonia, pneumonia, or old age. They rarely test for flu or other seasonal infections. If the patient has, say, cancer, motor neuron disease or another serious disease, this will be recorded as the cause of death, even if the final illness was a respiratory infection. This means UK certifications normally under record deaths due to respiratory infections.

Now, look at what has happened since the emergence of Covid-19. The list of notifiable diseases has been updated. The list which includes conditions like smallpox (which has been extinct for many years) as well as anthrax, brucellosis, the plague and rabies (which most UK doctors will never see in their entire careers) has now been amended to include Covid-19. But not flu. That means every positive test for Covid-19 must be notified, in a way that it just would not be for flu or most other infections.

2. **Dr John Oxford** is an English virologist and Professor at Queen Mary, University of London. He is a leading expert and voice on influenza, including bird flu, the 1918 Spanish Influenza, and HIV/AIDS.

This is what he says:

> *"Personally, I would say the best advice is to spend less time watching TV news which is sensational and not very good. Personally, I view this Covid outbreak as akin to a bad winter influenza epidemic. In this case we have had 8000 deaths this last year in the 'at risk' groups viz over 65% people with heart disease etc. I do not feel this current Covid will exceed this number. We are suffering from a media epidemic!"*

3. **Professor Knut Wittkowski** is German-American researcher and professor of epidemiology. He worked for 15 years on the Epidemiology of HIV before heading in the Department of Biostatistics, Epidemiology, and Research Design at The Rockefeller University in New York.

He says:

> *"With all respiratory diseases, the only thing that stops the disease is herd immunity. About 80% of the people need to have had contact with the virus, and the majority of them won't even have recognized that they were infected, or they had very, very mild symptoms, especially if they are children. So, it's very important to keep the schools open and kids mingling to spread the virus to get herd immunity as fast as possible.*
>
> *We are experiencing all sorts of counterproductive consequences of not well-thought-through policy*
>
> *I have been an epidemiologist for 35 years, and I have been modeling epidemics for 35 years. It's a pleasure to have the ability to help people to understand, but it's a struggle to get heard."*

4. **Dr Klaus Püschel** is German forensic pathologist and former professor of Forensics at Essen University. He is currently director of the Institute of Forensic Medicine at the University Medical Center, Hamburg-Eppendorf. He has worked on many noteworthy

autopsies, as well as high-profile forensic archaeological studies.

Contrary to the guidelines of the Robert Koch Institute, his office in Hamburg has started to differentiate between deaths *with* and *from* coronavirus, which led to a decrease in Covid-19 deaths.

What he says:

> *"This virus influences our lives in a completely excessive way. This is disproportionate to the danger posed by the virus. And the astronomical economic damage now being caused is not commensurate with the danger posed by the virus. I am convinced that the Corona mortality rate will not even show up as a peak in annual mortality.*
>
> *All those we have examined so far had cancer, a chronic lung disease, were heavy smokers or severely obese, suffered from diabetes or had a cardiovascular disease. The virus was the last straw that broke the camel's back, so to speak. Covid-19 is a fatal disease only in exceptional cases, but in most cases it is a predominantly harmless viral infection."*

He also made this statement:

> *"In quite a few cases, we have also found that the current corona infection has nothing whatsoever to*

> *do with the fatal outcome because other causes of death are present, for example, a brain haemorrhage or a heart attack. [Covid19 is] not particularly dangerous viral disease. All speculations about individual deaths that have not been expertly examined only fuel anxiety."*

5. **Dr Alexander Kekulé** is a German doctor and biochemist. He has held the Chair for Medical Microbiology and Virology at Martin Luther University Halle-Wittenberg since 1999 and is the current Director of the Institute for Medical Microbiology at the University Hospital Halle.

What he says:

> *"It's impossible to wait for a vaccine [...] The quickest we could have a vaccine ready is in six months. Based on experience, I'd say the reality is closer to a year. We can't stay under lockdown for six months to a year. If we did that our society and our culture would be ruined.*
>
> *People under 50 are very, very unlikely to die or get seriously ill from the coronavirus. We have to let them get infected so they can develop immunity."*

6. **Dr Claus Köhnlein** is a German Internist based in Kiel and co-author of the book 'Virus Mania'.

He says:

> *"[The coronavirus test] is a PCA-based test, where false positives are programmed in.*
>
> *Half of [the positive tests] could be wrong. PCA tests often show false positives. You can ask professor Gigerenzer in Berlin about this problem area. The tests are very sensitive. If you have only one molecule of something, the test can show positive. That doesn't mean the patient is sick, or that he has the coronavirus; it doesn't get isolated, but one relies wholly on these tests.*
>
> *At the moment one can't say how high the mortality rate really is, we need significantly more testing and significantly more sick or deceased people. It is too soon.*
>
> *But the spreading panic is in large parts founded on news from Italy. And nowadays one doesn't know how much of it is fake news. I have seen Italian doctors online, where I have compelling suspicions something isn't right with what they say.*
>
> *I am a clinician and I don't see a new disease on the horizon. If you took away the test, life would go on as before, there wouldn't be anything to see."*

7. **Dr Gérard Krause** is head of the Department for Epidemiology at the Helmholtz Centre for Infection in Braunschweig, director of the Institute for Infectious Disease Epidemiology at TWINCORE in Hannover, and Chair of the PhD Program Epidemiology at the

Hannover Medical School. He also coordinates the Translational Infrastructure Epidemiology at the German Centre for Infection Research (DZIF).

He states:

> *"We have to keep these serious social measures as short and as low as possible, because they could potentially cause more illnesses and deaths than the coronavirus itself.*
>
> *Although my focus is on infectious diseases, I believe that it is imperative that we consider the impact on other areas of health and society. We as a society must not focus solely on the victims of the corona virus.*
>
> *We know that unemployment, for example, causes illness and even increased mortality. It can also drive people into suicide. Restricting freedom of movement is likely to have a further negative impact on public health.*
>
> *It is not so easy to calculate such consequences directly, but they still happen and they can possibly be more serious than the consequences of the infections themselves."*

181

8. **Dr Gerd Gigerenzer** is a German psychologist, Professor of Psychology and Director of the Harding Center for Risk Literacy at the Max Planck Institute for Human Development in Berlin.

He says:

> *"The 2009 swine flu epidemic killed hundreds of thousands, mostly in Africa and Southeast Asia. But in Europe, where the threat was comparatively small, the media updated the death toll and the number of suspected cases on a daily basis.*
>
> *In the United Kingdom, the government predicted that as many as 65,000 citizens might die from the disease. In the end, fewer than 500 died.*
>
> *Predictably, such daily accounting triggered fear and led politicians to make hasty, ill-advised decisions – such as stockpiling medication – without examining the evidence.*
>
> *All eyes were focused on the new, unknown virus, and not on protecting people from more lethal threats, such as seasonal influenza, which in 2009 killed orders of magnitude more people than swine flu. It still does – as would be clear if the media bombarded us with hourly updates of the flu-related death toll.*
>
> *Similarly, millions of people, particularly in developing countries, die from malaria and tuberculosis each year. And in the United States alone, hospital-acquired infections kill some 99,000 patients annually. Yet, these unlucky people get next to no attention.*

> *Why are we more scared of what is less likely to kill us?*
>
> *[W]hen swine flu spread, many governments followed the World Health Organization's advice and stockpiled Tamiflu, a medication that was marketed to protect against the severe consequences of flu.*
>
> *Yet, **many expert advisers to the WHO had financial ties to drug manufacturers, and there is still no evidence that Tamiflu is effective.** The US wasted over $1 billion, and the UK over £400,000 ($522,000), on this medication – money that instead could have been invested in improving healthcare."*

These are top voices and leading experts giving different opinions about what is happening. I'll leave you to think about what they had to say.

In this next BONUS CHAPTER, you are going to learn the dark secrets of why all this is happening. I unravelled the truth that very few people will be willing to admit. I have unearthed ugly intentions, dark associations, and evil plans and schemes perpetrated by some of the most powerful people in the world. Unknown to the world and completely hidden from our eyes, details are laid bare all in this bonus chapter.

CHAPTER 9A

FROM A CRAZY MAN'S PERSPECTIVE!

Anishnabe prophecy: "There will come to a fork on the road. One road will lead to materialism and destruction...for all most all living creatures. The other road will lead to spirtitual way upon which the native people will be standing...this path will lead to the lightening of the 8th fire, a period of eternal peace, harmony and a "new earth" where the destruction of the past will heal."

We all see things differently but in life. We generally have two types of people: shepherds and sheeple. The shepherds tend to lead, whilst the sheeple usually graze and follow. Which one are you? Are you the type of individual who questions what they read, see and hear? Critically analyzing the data to obtain the TRUTH? Or are you the type of individual who takes what is fed to them by the popular media or even hearsay? How do YOU keep YOURSELF INFORMED in this LIFE? WHERE do YOU get YOUR NEWS and HOW? Do YOU get it first hand, second hand, third hand or more?

What I am going to discuss here you may never find anywhere within mainstream media. But it does not mean it is not correct. Do you understand? This may be OUTFORMATION to some of YOU (information that is out of your current world[s]).

COVID-19 STINKS to me. It SMELLS of Bill Gates, George Soros, Fauci, DEEP State, Big Pharma, Johnson and Johnson and CO. REALLY! Name me one person you personally know who has died of COVID-19? If WE put it to the TEST, despite ALL BIG MEDIA is SAYING I'm pretty sure that we wouldn't find any.

SEE!

....but there is more.

There are so many things going on in the world today, many bad. Well bad to us but not to the hands that do. Coronavirus is just one small part of it. Is it fact or is it fiction? I am sure that you have all made up your mind by now but I would just like to show you one more side.

In this life, most things that are happening around us do not happen by accident. Look at 9/11 for instance, was that an accident? Was the killing of Sadam Hussain an accident? Or was Ebola, Swine Flu, and Mers accidents? I will let you decide.

Experience tells me that hardly anything in our lives comes about by chance or accident. Has coronavirus (COVID-19) come around by chance or is it a result of a hidden agenda?

AGENDA is the keyword.

Before they were working towards AGENDA 21, AGENDA 30, AGENDA 60 and the CAMELOT PROJECT. That is not to mention Sustainable Development Goals signed off by the United Nations in 2015. Based on the ignorance of Medical Doctors on the immune system and nutrition, it looks like the UN planned to use coronavirus as a hidden enemy to scare the hell out of us in order to mandate vaccinations for the "common good."

All in the name of GOOD, they say. Well, that is the official narrative. And what about AGENDA **ID2020?**

An alliance of public and private partners, including UN agencies and civil society. It's an electronic ID program that uses generalized vaccination as a platform for digital identity.

This has been in consideration for many years with the final decision to go ahead taken in January 2020 at the World Economic Forum (WEF) in Davos. The Gates, GAVI (an association of vaccination-promoting pharmaceuticals), Rockefellers, Rothschilds *et al.*, are all behind this decision – the implementation of Agenda ID2020. Don't just believe me, please LOOK into all these things for yourself.

Have you noticed that they have tried a whole load of different tactics to covertly push through their agendas under the guise of such themes as, sustainability, environmentalism, and climate change?

What next? Is it going to be some BIG bonuses for BIG PHARMA?

Forced vaccinations?

Martial law?

What type of cocktails will be put into these vaccines?

- A slow killer that acts-up only in a few years
- A disease that hits only the next generation
- A brain debilitating agent
- Or a gene that renders men or women infertile

And what will be the hidden purpose of these vaccines?

- Population control
- Population reduction
- Genoicde
- Cashless society

How far are we going to let them take it?

And who are they?

Good question.

CHAPTER 9B

WELCOME TO THE DARKSIDE!

"The best slaves are the ones who do not realize that they are slaves." - Unknown

The WORLD as we know it is a reflection of us. WHATEVER has happened is down to us AS WE LET IT HAPPEN!

It may not be popular what I am going to say. It may not be believed. But I would like to show you a few things which I have found out on the way. Take it how you wish and take from it as you will.

WE ARE IN A WAR and have been for some TIME NOW. Since 2008 I SEE it, some would say from 2012.

WHY ARE WE IN LOCKDOWN? IS IT BECAUSE OF THE VIRUS THAT THEY MADE UP? Who has been running this PLANET or should WE more correctly say this PLAN-E.T? THEY were given 6000 years to get things right under certain conditions and they FAILED. There allotted TIME is now over. It ended officially on June 6, 1996. THEY KNOW. But they are REFUSING to RELINQUISH POWER, which kind of makes sense. WOULD YOU WANT to give up the RULERSHIP of this PLAN-E.T. if you were them?

WE are to blame as WE should be ready to take over the RUNNING of THINGS. But MOST of US are not READY for this as WE have been ENJOYING the benefits of an easy life under the PRESENT system that WE ARE LIVING – maritime law. Most of US do not LIKE to THINK for OURSELVES, most of US do not CRITICALLY analyze, TAKE responsibility or even ask QUESTIONS.

BABIES are dying every day, tortured, screaming for their lives. ADRENOCRHOME is the NAME. ABANDONED, NEGLECTED CHILDREN is the GAME. Ask MR EPSTEIN, MR PODESTA and MR SAVILLE what they have been PEDDLING. And, ask them how and why you would be interested to know.

Ask TOM HANKS why his INSTAGRAM LOOKS kind of creepy and strange, with images of gloves and shoes of little boys and girls, odd gloves, odd shoes, cryptic sick messages and sometimes blood? There have been RUMORS that he was PUT on HOUSE ARREST recently, but nothing was published in the media, but they did REPORT that he was QUARANTINED with CORONAVIRUS? Who KNOWS?

Apparantly, the QUEEN of ENGLAND loves ADRENOCHROME but I am sure that she would never admit this. She hasn't even admitted that her CORONATION was FAKE. Nor has she explained how a naked child plunged to his death after been seen scaling bedsheets trying to escape from Buckingham Palace. This is all common knowledge. Google "naked immigrant dies at Buckingham Palace" and you will SEE. FAKE NEWS THEY SAY! REALLY?

What about the DEATH of PRINCESS DIANA, didn't that LEAVE a bad smell in the air for a WHILE? Did YOU KNOW what the ETYMOLOGY of the word QUEEN is? YOU will be very surprised.

QUEEN = SLUT.

Check it out for YOURSELF. WE DON'T NEED TITLES BECAUSE WE ARE GODS.

Check out PSALMS 82 verse 6 when you get chance.

ALL these THINGS go on every day, while most of US WALK around as if everything is ok? To ME EVERYTHING is NOT OK, but ALL is good. THIS PLAN-E.T. will be CLEANSED soon, sometime before 2038. But it is really hard to calculate and know the things working off this FAKE TIME that most of us are involved with.

WE ALL need to attune ourselves back into natural time. There are many books on this I suggest you read up on it and adjust yourself accordingly. Check out my book 'CHOICES 3,' I have written up on the subject of TIME, but there have been many masters before me who have already dealt with the topic.

It is the END of an experiment that was done on Earth. An end to the allowed time for the Annunakis and Reptilians as some would call them in ruling this world. I do not SEE it LIKE this. I SEE the ROMAN CATHOLICS and JESUITS are the ones RUNNING the SHOW who were given a set time to rule, a set time to master the waters and the skies. THEY FAILED, THEY DIDN'T DO IT as YOU CAN SEE.

The problem is that these people are only good for managing populations up to around 500,000,000 people. Today's population is going on its way to 8 billion, despite all the genocide. They also do evil things all in the name of 'GOOD.' They WILL do anything to PROTECT their ORDER which is VERY NOBLE. It is a shame that WE are not the same. Check out Appendix 1 when you get chance, I have left you some stuff to read which will open your eyes a bit.

MANY of YOU will not SEE it. Many of YOU WILL not KNOW it. EVEN when I tell you, you may well be the same. That is the SPELL! The ILLUSION! The MAGIC! Most people THINK that it is ALL about RELIGION, POLITICS and SCIENCE. They are WRONG. That is NOTHING. MAGIC is KEY.

ALCHEMY is the ONLY THING that COUNTS in the GRAND scheme of THINGS, LAW and COMMERCE ASIDE. ALCHEMY is the makeup of ALL THINGS. Just like CHEMISTRY is the makeup of all MINERAL COMPOSITES. WE HUMANS are made UP of 102 minerals I am an ALIEN I KNOW. YOU are PROBABLY one also. I am in this WORLD but not of it or from it.

We ALL have GALACTIC ORIGINS. We are all originally from either Pleiades, Atlantia, Sirius, Lemur, Andromeda, Alpha Centauri, Arcturus, Mushaba, etc. My family are originally from the SIRIUS STAR CONSTELLATION. I am a STAR CHILD or STAR SEED. Where are you and YOUR FAMILY FROM? Do YOU KNOW? It will be encoded in YOUR DNA, for SURE. In every human DNA is an embedded code that identifies the true heritage of every single human being.

195

We were the first people on this planet – everybody knows. WE had OUR HOLY LAND. ISRAEL – ISIS-RA-EL. But now everybody THINKS it is theirs. They are always fighting over it as YOU CAN SEE but I do not wish to get into that one. SO who is REALLY RUNNING the WORLD? Or who is TRYING to RUN the WORLD? Any IDEAS?

Let US continue this in the next chapter, I would just like to give you one extract to read before moving on, it is a little long but please stay with it, you cannot miss this KNOWLEDGE, this must stop, now.

Let US SEE how DEEP this RABBIT HOLE really is
PLEASE SEE BELOW:

"EXPLOSIVE: Pedophile Ring Linked To Adrenochrome Drug Trafficking

I've been watching social media for a couple of days and noticed today the term "LOLITA EXPRESS" was trending on Twitter. I found that somewhat interesting since there's been a lot of talk about sex scandals recently even in the mainstream news.

About a year ago, I did a story on Pizzagate and some wanted to just push it to the side and say it's ridiculous, however, since this is once again the topic of discussion, we've uncovered some more evidence pointing to the reality of child sex trafficking, abuse and murder which might put some of this in perspective if that term can even be used in this twisted depravity plaguing our government and the world.

Much of this story started out with the publishing of John Podesta's emails by Wikileaks. The reason these are important is because Podesta was Hillary Clinton's Campaign Chairman during her failed attempt at taking over our government.

Wikileaks has a track record of 100 percent accuracy in its documents which makes it even more important to study what's going on between Hillary, her friends, her associates and her campaign.

Within those emails, there are hundreds of pedophile references including something called Spirit Cooking which many of us didn't even know existed until this document dump.

Once this was uncovered, we were led to a highly unusual involvement with the Democrats and a place called Comet Ping Pong and it's owner James Alefantis. Some speculate this guy is part of the Rothschild's – and there's even a Pastebin dump from a hacker pointing to Alefantis's relationship with the Rothschild's.

However, on the bottom of the Pastebin dump, there is a reference that Alefantis has a connection to biochemistry. Online postings say Alefantis dropped out of college. Maybe he did. He seems like an ordinary Street Thug, dealer who is hooked up in deviant activity but just slick enough to make sure he doesn't get pinned with any more connection to pedophilia than is necessary to maintain his business which I believe involves child sex trafficking and the sale of something called Adrenochrome.

Adrenochrome is mentioned in the movie "Fear and Loathing in Las Vegas" starring Johnny Depp and if you watch this quick clip to the end, it talks about this drug. Take a look.

In this clip, it's interesting to note the discussion between Depp and the Dealer he's talking to. If you didn't realize it, they're talking about how it's harvested in around about way.

Yes, I'm well aware this is supposed to be fiction, however most fiction is based on real life events. Authors do a lot of research on their subjects and this movie isn't about Depp going down the rabbit hole or making chocolate in a make believe factory.

This is much closer to real life than people would like to admit.

Adrenochrome is a chemical produced by the human body when adrenaline (or epinephrine) oxidizes or "hits the air." It's produced when the body is traumatized in some way such as through torture or extreme terror.

When a stimulus which should produce extreme fear is introduced to a human, especially when someone is very young, the adrenaline produced is more potent than the average adult. Because of it's psychoactive properties Adrenochrome has been linked to mind control drug. Think MK Ultra.

The extraction process is done by killing the person and harvesting the adrenochrome from the base of the neck and spinal column with a needle.

In its pure form, black market dealers can make extreme amounts of money when they sell it. This connection between the child sex trafficking, torture and murder of children around the world and the links between MS-13, high profile pedopushers like Podesta and Alefantis and all the ties between these non-profit organizations pretending to provide assistance to victims of various disasters around the world makes sense when you think about this type of drug trafficking.

What better way to collect children than from war torn or natural disaster ripped areas? Parents are gone, families are separated. It's too easy to get these kid in and out of the country. They slap a few faces of children on their posters and then no one ever really tracks the kids after a certain point.

And there's also a site online from Canada called Androchrome Labs dot com which says it manufactures it's own product and sells it in vape form. Seems pretty interesting they're using vaporizers now to cover their drug pushing. This isn't regulated and isn't in a "food form" so it doesn't have to go through the FDA for approval.

Look at this company in Germany. It's called Gute Chemie which does say it sells Adrenochrome in their catalog — pricing on request.

OK so here's some of the side effects related to the use of Adrenochrome directly from the "addiction library dot org"

An Adrenochrome user may experience euphoria, confusion, a change in train of thought, lack of judgment, poor insight and inability to concentrate. It also says on this site, those who use it may become dependent on it and feel as if they can't function without it.

Since it's unregulated in the United States and isn't approved for human consumption, distribution isn't tough and getting caught with it, isn't a crime.

The very existence of this drug has been debated however, it seems odd, if it didn't exist, why is it on the Addiction Library site with it's definition, how it's used, what the signs and symptoms of it's use are and how to treat those addicted, if it wasn't real?

If you connect what we know about the pedophile rings in PizzaGate, Alefantis, the connection between Wikileaks, John Podesta, Tony Podesta, their relationship with Alefantis, the artwork in Tony's house, the trails from the Lolita Express, the round up of MS-13 and the connects between this and the so-called Blue Bloods and all of these sealed indictments, the sex scandals and pedophilia in politics and on and on and on, it looks as if, Alefantis is neck deep into this particular aspect of criminal activity by supplying a trafficking hub for the exchange of kidnapped children and pushing the drug Adrenochrome.

We know he's involved — it's too obvious — there's just too much evidence supporting his involvement but now we know why. It makes too much sense.

So when Alefantis lawyers and Podesta's lawyers and anyone else who wants to send a "cease and desist" letter to me decides they don't like us talking about the connections to this deviant and evil behavior, I'll post it as I normally do when I get letters like this.

Note to lawyers — you might just want to save the paper. It makes pretty pictures for my walls.

In the next few days, we've got some pretty big stories coming your way including the connection between Uranium One and Canada which I see the main stream media is starting to cover,

as well as some recent raids by the FBI on several banking facilities including one really small bank which has a portfolio of about 1.4 Billion dollars in the middle of nowhere and employs about 40 people. There assets seem to be frozen.

Then one of our big stories which is about Mandalay Bay, the FBI connection and how ISIS gun running is connected to this story.

All this and more next week. Keep watching and sending me information. We're weeding through it as fast as we can but it's just me and a couple of people here.

Thanks to all the people donating to our site and endeavors and I'll try to get another video out for you who are waiting for more information on the financial side of the deception perpetrated on us by the government.

As always, keep vigilant!

Sources/References:

Andrenochrome Lab:
https://www.abcr.de/shop/en/catalogsearch/advanced/result/?q=adrenochrome

Addition Library:
https://addictionlibrary.org/illicit/adrenochrome-uses-symptoms-signs-addiction-treatment.html

Postbin:
http://archive.is/ZNm9y"[53]

DID YOU KNOW ABOUT ANY OF THIS STUFF? And WE SUPPORT THESE PEOPLE in POWER? REALLY?

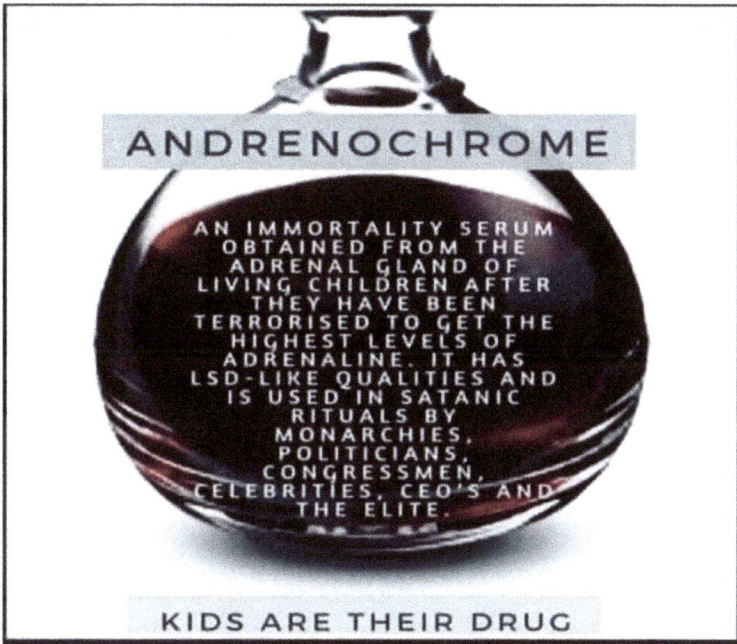

ANDRENOCHROME

AN IMMORTALITY SERUM OBTAINED FROM THE ADRENAL GLAND OF LIVING CHILDREN AFTER THEY HAVE BEEN TERRORISED TO GET THE HIGHEST LEVELS OF ADRENALINE. IT HAS LSD-LIKE QUALITIES AND IS USED IN SATANIC RITUALS BY MONARCHIES, POLITICIANS, CONGRESSMEN, CELEBRITIES, CEO'S AND THE ELITE.

KIDS ARE THEIR DRUG

Adrenochrome The Elites Super Drug | Follow The White Rabbit

100,774 views • Mar 25, 2020

2K   50   SHARE   SAVE   ...

---

53 https://aprillajune.com/explosive-pedophile-ring-linked-adrenochrome-drug-trafficking/ accessed April 26th 2020 @14:14

Adrenochrome is only produced from adrenaline that is pumped out of fear, gives you quicker reactions, elevated senses and strength etc. which is why they must be alive

			2015 Pop	Missing kids
1	1	California	39,144,818	592
2	2	Texas	27,469,114	327
3	4	Florida	20,271,272	355
4	3	New York	19,795,791	203
5	5	Illinois	12,859,995	135
6	6	Pennsylvania	12,802,503	112
7	7	Ohio	11,613,423	122
8	9	Georgia	10,214,860	92
9	10	North Carolina	10,042,802	68
10	8	Michigan	9,922,576	92
11	11	New Jersey	8,958,013	59
12	12	Virginia	8,382,993	392

ALABAMA'S MISSING
BUT
NOT FORGOTTEN

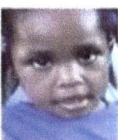

Stephanie Elizabeth Condon | Rachel Louise Cooke | Kiplyn Davis | Asha Jaquilla Degree | Georgina DeJesus | Diamond Yvette Bradley

Trenton John Duckett | Jaycee Lee Dugard | Benjamin Everett | Kaelin Rose Glazier | Blanca Lillian Campos | Chioma Gray

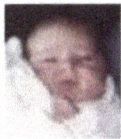

Jamie Harper | Shausha Latine Henson | Sofia Lucerno Juarez | Rolando Salas Jusino | Shaina Ashley Kirkpatrick | Steven Earl Kraft, Jr.

Bianca Lebron | Brianna Maitland | Bethany Leanne Markowski | Kristen Modafferi | Alexis S. Patterson | Bianca Noel Piper

Kemberly Ramer | Bryan Dos Santos-Gomez | Kristin Denise Smart | Reachelle Smith | Tionda Z. Bradley | Khoi Dang Vu

205

Source: 54

time. The subject is sometimes kept alive for numerous extractions. **The way it's done is through a needle being punctured into the eye to secret adrenaline/epinephrine from the brain stem.**

Adrenochrome Harvesting and The Elite

The Elite are said to run massive child trafficking rings all around the world, buying and selling children for their own pleasure. Children are heavily used since they experience a huge spike of adrenaline from the pineal gland. In 2018, NCMEC reports 424,000+ missing children every year in America.

A lot of the Elite are addicted to the substance. They participate in what is called 'Spirit Cooking' and have parties surrounding on the subject of human sacrificing. **These people sacrifice children, eat the bodies, drink the blood and worship dark gods.** This stuff tends to be quite addicting. Many who try the drug tend to have a hard time coming off it.

One prime example of the Elite and the famous drug is the example of Al Gore. Al Gore

---

54 https://www.youtube.com/watch?feature=share&v
=rBH5wPQrWIY&fbclid=IwAR0EahOl2IZVmg9LMZ4ONfx4L
ptQ-FxnwtKBQrolC-aWMT5yhefoQFK1X8Y&app=desktop
accessed May 5th 2020 @23:52

Adrenochrome is said to cause **mental disorders, derealisation, and euphoria**.

How is Adrenochrome Harvested?

Adrenochrome is said to be harvested from kidnapped children under the age of 9 (the drug is more potent). The children need to be at their most fearful in order to extract potent adrenaline/epinephrine from their pineal gland. It has the combined effects of both super strong speed and LSD.

The adrenaline/epinephrine is extracted quickly as the adrenaline is not as potent over time. The subject is sometimes kept alive for numerous extractions. **The way it's done is through a needle being punctured into the eye to secret adrenaline/epinephrine from the brain stem**.

I wouldn't know personally, but evidence suggests that adrenochrome is a most sought after drug amongst the rich famous and superwealthy. It has also been linked to mind control because of its psychoactive properties (such as MK Ultra).

I don't want to go into it too much but I didn't want to miss it either, as whilst technically it is sold legally, it is highly unethical and immoral as the extraction process is done by killing a frightened child and harvesting the adrenochrome from the base of the neck and spinal column with a needle, the more scared and tortured the child, the better the drug. In it's pure form, black market dealers can make extreme amounts of money when they sell it as they do.

Red wine is symbolic of the blood ingestedLuciferiansians and satanist when they are doing there rituals. What about the wine we all drink? The wine can become sanctified as it did in the Roman

207

Catholic Church, a patsy for the Reptilians. In the Catholic Church, wine often replaced the blood in ceremony. You may have seen this before. Have you ever been to church and had communion where they bring red wine to drink with bread. We all love drinking the wine in church... mmmhh, very nice. Little did we know that we were carrying out a symbolic satanic ritual as if we are savouring on blood and flesh (we may as well be at bohemian grove ourselves). I suggest you look into all these things PROPERLY yourself - YOU MAY BE SURPRISED.

Whatever happened to EPSTEIN? Some say he isn't dead? But some people also say that Tupac and Elvis are not really dead? What do YOU THINK? And whatever happened to Harvey WEINSTEIN? YOU KNOW that guy? Why didn't he go to PRISON for his CRIMES AGAINST HUMANITY? All those poor young girls. $25,000,000 and a bit of shame sorted that one out. Don't these guys just get off nicely!? Maybe I should change my name to EILSTEIN... I might get a pass.

Interestingly, adrenochrome has been commercially available from the city of Wuhan in China for many years. Wuhan, as you know, is where the COVID-19 virus allegedly originated.

CHAPTER 9C

SUB PLOT!

"We the people "ARE THE SOLUTION" to our problems. Do not wait for help when our lesson is to help ourselves!"

– Bernadette Gervais Greene

So WHO REALLY is RUNNING the WORLD? Everyone has their own IDEAS. I have mine. I am not going to provide any references but I am going to try and explain some stuff. Take it as YOU MAY! Some may SEE it as FANTASY, FICTION where others may SEE it as FACTION, DIVINE TRUTH.Who KNOWS do YOU?

So who REALLY RUNS the WORLD? In this day and age, everyone has an opinion who rules? Some would say it's the **Democrats** or the **Republicans**, others would say it's the **Globalists or the Elite**. Some say that it is the **Illuminati** or the **Freemasons** and then there is the group who thinks the **Jews run the world.**

What is a JEW? What does it mean? What is Semitic? What is Anti-Semitic? Let us leave this talk for another day.

NO!

LET'S DO IT NOW! RIGHT NOW!

A Jew is a Greek-Egyptian (Gews, Jews). They stole all of the sciences from the African peoples via Pheonician Egyptians who preceded them. I am pretty sure that Moshe Rabbenu will remember this. The Greek Jews were taught by the Phoenician-Egyptians, and they were taught by the Ethiopians-Egyptians/Africans. Check all it out you will SEE for YOURSELF!

Now let US LOOK into a couple of definitions:

*"**Semitic | Definition of Semitic by Merriam-Webster***

Semitic definition is - of, relating to, or constituting a subfamily of the Afro-Asiatic language family that includes Hebrew, Aramaic, Arabic, and Amharic."[55]

---

55   https://www.merriam-webster.com/dictionary/Semitic accessed May 11th 2020 @11:24

"**_Anti-semitic | Definition of Anti-semitic by Merriam-Webster_**

Anti-Semitic definition is - relating to or characterized by anti-Semitism : feeling or showing hostility toward or discrimination against Jews as a cultural, racial, or ethnic group." [56]

Need I say more? It is funny how the definitions are not the opposite of each other. Is it not? Before WE start let US have a LOOK at this PICTURE, it always seems to make OUR LIVES easier. It would SEEM that ALL ROADS LEAD to ROME!

SO WHO IS REALLY RUNNING THE WORLD?

You thought you were pretty well informed about what is going on in this WORLD? You may have noticed the various elements of society who control our world from behind the scenes or the role played by the banking CARTEL.

(211)

Organizations such as the CFR (Council on Foreign Relations), the Trilateral Commission, the Bilderbergers, the Committee of 300 (the 17 wealthiest so-called "elite" families)—the Rothschilds in England and Rockefellers in America and Bronfmans

---

56

https://duckduckgo.com/?q=semetic&t=palemoon&ia=de finition accessed May 11th 2020 @11:26

in Canada and so on, comprising the physical power structure of the New World Order puppets under the direction of darkly motivated, other-dimensional "master deceivers" commonly known as Lucifer or Satan and their "fallen angel" cohorts.

But this is not even half the story.

There is so much more.

The other side of the story is so well hidden from general public view. I wonder why?

> *"These are the ones who claim to be "Jews", but are NOT "Jews". They are the worshippers of Satan, and are his chosen seed line on this earth to do HIS WILL, even as we are Jah's chosen people called to do His."*
> *- Rev 2:9 & 3:9*

This passage in the bible explains what has been going on on this PLAN-E.T. for the last 6,500 years. It is plain to SEE that things have not been right. WE have the ones who claim to be JEWS at WAR with JAH's chosen people. This is what has been going on! I will elaborate as we go through this chapter.

Fortunately, for me, I am not from any of these bloodlines as my story and family bloodline goes back millions of years. But WE are still stuck in the middle of everything, which is not good. Not at ALL! WAR has been affecting everyone on the PLAN-E.T. WE get to EXPERIENCE the SIDE EFFECTS, lucky us. MOST OF

US, have been LIVING in a 3D REALITY for most of OUR LIVES under the pretext of two polarities: **GOOD** and EVIL!

GOD and THE DEVIL or LUCIFER or SATAN as some would say. These are the two **POWERS**, the **FORCES** of **GOOD** and EVIL! At present, it appears that Lucifer/Satan has the world in its EVIL grip. **BUT FOR HOW LONG? SO WHO IS REALLY RUNNING THE WORLD? WELL, IT IS NOT GOD. NO, IT IS NOT THE GODS! YOU SEE!**

EVERYTHING in this LIFE is about ENERGY, POSITIVE, and NEGATIVE. From this 3D perspective, WE tend to deal with POLARITES: NORTH and SOUTH POLE; POSITIVE and NEGATIVE.

For the past 6,500 years, a very EVIL FORCE has been DOMINATING WORLD AFFAIRS, CONTROLLING the WORLD as WE SPEAK. FROM GOD's SEAT on the PLAN-E.T. The SEAT for the MOST HIGH is CURRENTLY being OCCUPIED by one of the MOST LOW. IMAGINE THAT?

213

Everything starts with Lucifer/Satan. The Appendix takes you deeper into the evil machination that is going in the world. Case studies are being discussed. All the details are verifiable facts online. Stories that you have probably not heard before are now told. You are in for a shock in the appendix. Take note: this book is a life manual because this is just the beginning. Arm yourself with the truth.

CONCLUSION

THE FINAL CALL

This is a final call for responsibility. To stand up against tyranny. To take your own destiny and that of your family in your own hands. I can't unearth was is going on in a book. No matter what happens, remember something:

MAN WILL ALWAYS WIN

https://www.facebook.com/kacpermp/videos/2463114 03276247/UzpfSTEwMDAwMDA5NjAzNTQzMTozMzY 5NDE5NTE5NzM3ODgz/?lst=551544458%3A10000009 6035431%3A1589570001

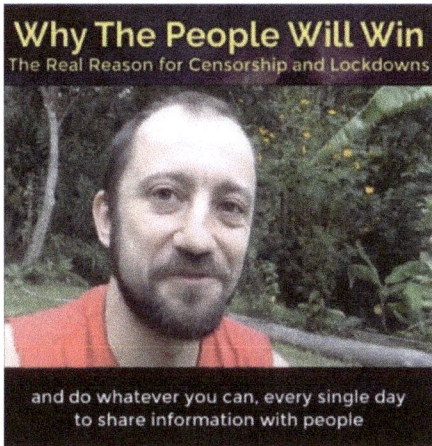

Why The People Will Win
The Real Reason for Censorship and Lockdowns

and do whatever you can, every single day
to share information with people

As I have buttressed several times in this book. Everything was strategically planned. It has been planned for years. How did CNN know about it? They reported it as far back as 12th of March 2018.

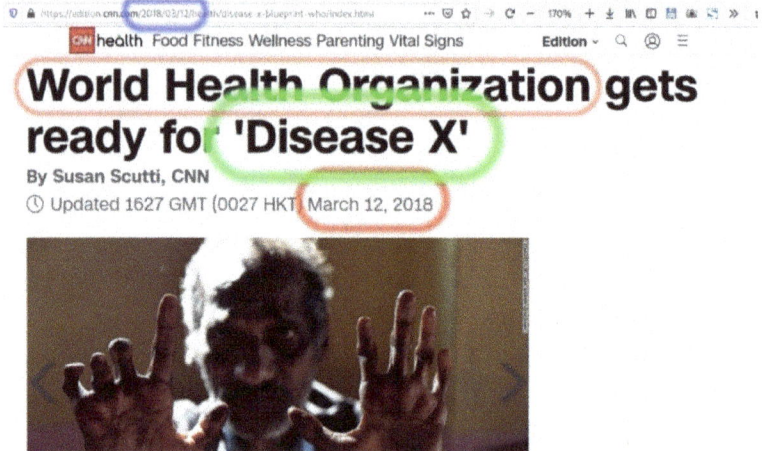

CoViD19

$1 + 9 = 10$

ten = X

They knew in 2018 about the global plan.

CNN, 12th of March, 2018

And a patent application from Wuhan occurred at almost the same time.

5. CN107245095 - POLYPEPTIDE INHIBITOR FOR INHIBITING TEN CORONA VIRUSES

Patent application in 2017 from Wuhan University. Followed by the the WHO announcing a year later that "Disease X" is coming.

X = ten

In early 2020, "COVID-19" emerges from Wuhan, China.

1 + 9 = 10
10 = X

Virus = disease "COVID-19" is "disease X."

Do not be deceived, there is no war between China's 'deep state' and the 'deep state' of the US. Hong Kong is still effectively a shared asset between China and the Crown. World socialism, led by Rome, is rolling forward. Babylon is rising (yet has fallen). Powerful men want to depopulate the world and enforce their evil agenda. But it is your responsibility to stand up and say no TODAY!

COVID is an RNA structured virus and not a DNA structured virus.

So what is the difference between a DNA and RNA?

Deoxyribonucleic acid (DNA) and Ribonucleic acid (RNA) are perhaps the most important molecules in cell biology, responsible for the storage and reading of genetic information that underpins all life. They are both linear polymers, consisting of sugars, phosphates, and bases, but there are some key differences which separate the two.

218

DNA vs. RNA – A Comparison Chart

Comparison	DNA	RNA
Full Name	Deoxyribonucleic Acid	Ribonucleic Acid
Function	DNA replicates and stores genetic information. It is a blueprint for all	RNA converts the genetic information contained within DNA to

	genetic information contained within an organism	a format used to build proteins, and then moves it to ribosomal protein factories.
Structure	DNA consists of two strands, arranged in a double helix. These strands are made up of subunits called nucleotides. Each nucleotide contains a phosphate, a 5-carbon sugar molecule and a nitrogenous base.	RNA only has one strand, but like DNA, is made up of nucleotides. RNA strands are shorter than DNA strands. RNA sometimes forms a secondary double helix structure, but only intermittently.
Length	DNA is a much longer polymer than RNA. A chromosome, for example, is a single, long DNA molecule, which	RNA molecules are variable in length, but much shorter than long DNA polymers. A large RNA

	would be several centimeters in length when unraveled.	molecule might only be a few thousand base pairs long.
Sugar	The sugar in DNA is deoxyribose, which contains one less hydroxyl group than RNA's ribose.	RNA contains ribose sugar molecules, without the hydroxyl modifications of deoxyribose.
Bases	The bases in DNA are Adenine ('A'), Thymine ('T'), Guanine ('G') and Cytosine ('C').	RNA shares Adenine ('A'), Guanine ('G') and Cytosine ('C') with DNA, but contains Uracil ('U') rather than Thymine.
Base Pairs	Adenine and Thymine pair (A-T) Cytosine and Guanine pair (C-G)	Adenine and Uracil pair (A-U) Cytosine and Guanine pair (C-G)
Location	DNA is found in	RNA forms in

	the nucleus, with a small amount of DNA also present in mitochondria.	the nucleolus, and then moves to specialized regions of the cytoplasm depending on the type of RNA formed.
Reactivity	Due to its deoxyribose sugar, which contains one less oxygen–containing hydroxyl group, DNA is a more stable molecule than RNA, which is useful for a molecule which has the task of keeping genetic information safe.	RNA, containing a ribose sugar, is more reactive than DNA and is not stable in alkaline conditions. RNA's larger helical grooves mean it is more easily subject to attack by enzymes.
Ultraviolet (UV) Sensitivity	DNA is vulnerable to damage by ultraviolet light.	RNA is more resistant to damage from UV light than DNA.

So you can see that RNA is not structurally stable. Any virus that is RNA mutates or changes. So, you cannot have an effective vaccine for an RNA structured virus like HIV. It's the same thing with COVID-19. If you have noticed there are lots of different COVID symptoms. People might have diarrhoea, fever, headache, chest discomforts, loss of taste and smell, and so on. One person might have a single symptom, another might have a few, some may have no symptoms at all.

COVID is a virus that has affected most parts of the world, which is unlike naturally occurring viruses that spread over a specific region or space at a particular time. They have to breed and be effective in a particular climate and they are not so effective in other climates. Yes, naturally occurring viruses might later spread further afield but it does not happen simultaneously.

People behind this pandemic are trampling on our rights. As a matter of fact, this is a bigger threat than COVID-19 itself. The virus will go but these people will continue in their tyranny. People are subjected to staying at home; not being able to go out other than for a non-essential shop. Churches were shut for Easter Sunday and more than 23 million Americans have lost their jobs because they are deemed "non-essentials." Yet, the US government has spent more than 2 billion dollars on palliative measures. Like I said, there are more questions than answers.

Something very wrong is going on and you and I cannot afford to waste trying to find out.

What we have to do is to take cover. Protect ourselves and our families. Start an online business in case you lose your job and demand for what is right in the society.

I leave you with this message of hope and inspiration from a medical doctor operating in one of the cities experiencing a major battle with COVID-19 – New York. Listen to it and the message is DO NOT BE AFRAID.

https://web.facebook.com/watch/?v=517230645634788

But we are not yet finished.

You see, there is a principle of cause and effect.

The universal law of *cause and effect* states that for every **effect** there is a definite **cause**, likewise for every **cause**, there is a definite **effect**.

224

APPENDIX 1

ARTHUR NEUMANN aka Henry Deacon – All Interviews – Secret Space Program

February 17, 2013

NOTE: This page contains all written and video Camelot interviews with Arthur Neumann.

Re: Arthur Neumann is his real name. Initially, when he first came forward he did so under an assumed name, Henry Deacon, to protect himself and his family. In 2009, he decided to come forward under his real name.

projectcamelot.org/henry_deacon.html

This interview was transcribed from video as the interviewee expressed a wish to remain anonymous ('Henry Deacon' is a pseudonym, prompted by his similarity to the likeable and creative polymath on the *Eureka* TV series). Certain details have been deleted and/or amended in order to ensure that his identity remains concealed, and the transcript has been "cleaned" of most expressed natural hesitations and the like. Meanwhile, it is most important to note that none of the factual information disclosed has been altered or amended in any way.

Henry's name and employment details are known and verified and we were able to meet with him personally more than once. He was understandably a little nervous but definitely wanted to talk with us. In conversation, he sometimes responded with silence and meaningful glances or enigmatic smiles rather than words. He was entirely disarming, in a very quiet way, and was not always certain about what he should or shouldn't say. At times, however, he took great pleasure in revealing the truth about some key matter in a way that could not be traced back to him. One or two supplementary details were provided by e-mail after the interview.

The most important piece of additional information comes at the very end of the transcript, where Henry confirms Dan Burisch's testimony.

Readers are welcome to distribute this freely with the proviso that no part of it must be altered or deleted. Unaltered extracts can be quoted if the context is made clear. We consider this interview to be extremely important and in our opinion the information revealed should be made widely known.

We have heard nothing from Henry Deacon for the last five weeks. Prior to our last communication, in the last week of March 2007, he had told us he was being 'coerced'. Up to that time he had been in very regular communication with us. We now feel certain he has been forced into silence.

While this newest update contains fascinating further information on a number of topics (including more information on Mars and some details of the inside story of 9/11), we continue to believe that the most important information he has shared is to be found in the second update. However, as stated above, new readers are advised to read Henry's testimony in sequence.

227

Start of interview

Please tell us a little bit about yourself – as much as you feel you can.

I'm a current employee of one of the three-letter agencies [he plays a little word game with us until we guess the right agency, which he then confirms]. I'm probably taking quite a risk by speaking to you like this, though I don't intend to reveal any information that in my judgment is both classified and specific to national security. I've been involved in many projects with many different agencies over many years. To jump right in at the deep end, I believe I was a walk-in around eighth grade. I have memories of coming from another planet, and these are all mixed up, all mingled with human boyhood memories. It's very weird, and hard to explain what it feels like. I've never had any problems intuitively accessing complex scientific information and I've often found myself understanding complex systems with no detailed briefing or training. I work essentially with systems. I don't mean to be arrogant, but I do know a great deal of advanced information, scientific and otherwise. I just seem to know it. I can't say more than that right now.

Can you give even any clues about which agency you work for?

No, not on public record. I just can't afford that.

What information do you feel you have that's important for the world to know?

There's so much that it's hard to know where to start.I knew about 9/11 two years before the event, for instance. Not in specific terms, but certainly in general ones. It was talked about, an event like that, something that would change the game, let's say.I know that there's a planned war between the US and China scheduled for late 2008. This is also geopolitical and not concerned with Black Ops as such. These were both just events that I got to hear about in passing. I have no detailed information about them.

You mean that China and the US are working together to stage a war?

The Pentagon started the planning in 1998. You have to understand that China and the US are hand in glove with everything. This war is a joint op between the US and China. Most wars are set up that way and have been for a while. Do you want something else that's just unpleasant to hear? I also heard from someone who was serving in a unit that worked with missiles deployed for testing in the Pacific and the Far East. The missiles were shipped to the test location in very tightly sealed containers, very secure, hermetically sealed. After the tests, the container would be shipped back, sealed the same way, but empty, supposedly empty. On one occasion, this guy was present when a container was opened. It wasn't empty. It was filled with bags of white powder.

Cocaine?

I leave you to draw your own conclusions. I doubt it
was sugar. Let me just say that, hypothetically
speaking, and let me just say that to protect myself, if
such a plan was in operation, it makes perfect
logistical sense as it's a totally secure way to get
around all security, customs, international boundaries
and ports, and all those checks. It's perfect, like the
way guns and ammunition used to cross borders in
diplomatic bags going between consulates. This
happens all the time.

Would you call yourself a physicist?

Yes. I cover other specialities as well, but yes, I'm a
physicist. And I specialize in systems. Livermore is a
good place to be, everyone's very professional there.
They don't, you know, they don't play games there.

**What can you say about the current state of physics in
the military-industrial complex?**

It's dozens of years ahead of mainstream physics
which is published in journals in the public domain.
There are projects dealing with subjects beyond the
belief or experience, beyond the imagination, of many
public domain physicists.

Can you give us any examples?

[long pause] There's a project called Shiva Nova at
Livermore which uses arrays of giant lasers. These are

huge lasers, huge capacitors, many terawatts of energy, in a building built on giant springs [extends his arms to show the size], all focused on a tiny tiny point. This creates a fusion reaction which replicates certain conditions for nuclear weapons testing. It's like a nuke test in lab conditions, and there's very powerful data collection focused on that point where all the energy is focused. The problem is that all extremely high-energy events like this create rips in the fabric of spacetime. This was observed back in the early Hiroshima and Nagasaki events, and you can even see it in the old movies. Look for what looks like an expanding energy sphere, and I can send you a link to show you. The problem with creating rips in spacetime, whether they're big or little, is that things get in that you don't want to be there.

Things get in?

Things get in. Things that we all know about that are discussed on the net a lot. Beings, and influences, and all kinds of weird stuff, and I can tell you they've created big problems.

What kind of problems?

[pause]The problem of their presence and then what happens next. The other problem is that if you're creating rips in spacetime you're messing with time itself, whether you mean to or not. There have been attempts to fix that, and it all results in a complicated overlay of time loops. Some ETs are trying to help, and

others, others are not. When predicting futures, we can only talk about probable and possible futures. This is all extremely complex and very highly classified. Basically, it's just a huge mess. We've opened Pandora's Box, starting with the Manhattan Project, and we haven't yet found a way to deal with the consequences.

The problem of multiple timelines sounds like the information reported by Dan Burisch... can you comment on that?

[shakes head] I don't know about any of that.

OK. We'll send you the links so that you can see the interviews. But what you're saying also corroborates the information reported by "Mr X" on the Camelot website. Have you seen or read those interviews?

No, what does he say?

"Mr X" is an archivist who for six months had the opportunity to work with classified documents, films, photos and artifacts back in the mid-80s when he was working on a special project with a defense contractor. He says that he read that the principal reason for the ETs' interest in us was because of nuclear testing and the general threat of nuclear weapons.

That sounds about right. Except only one or two ET groups are concerned about nuclear weapons, not all of them.

OK. What else can you tell us about the timeline problem?

Just that it's unresolved. The risk is, you see, that each time we try to fix it, it adds to the problem. It just gets worse all the time.

Are the aliens – or some of the aliens – time travelers? Dan Burisch states this.

Yes.

Do you know about the Montauk Project?

That caused a huge problem, and generated a... created a 40-year loop.I don't know about Al Bielek. I believe some of his information is suspect. But something like that definitely did happen, the Philadelphia Experiment, too. John Neumann was very involved in all of that.

And Tesla, and Einstein?

Don't know. But Neumann... [nods head]

Montauk was real?

Yes. That was a real mess. They created a time split we're still unable to mend. Now, understand this also relates to Project Rainbow, the Stargates... they were also working on that there. But some of the Montauk reports on the net are unconvincing to me. I've seen some of the photos of the equipment they're supposed to have used, and it's junk, just a pile of junk.

[Bill] I've always had a problem with the idea of time portals because I don't see how or why they'd stay with the planet at a certain location as it moves through space. If a portal was created in spacetime, you'd expect it to be left behind somewhere very quickly as the earth rotates, and moves round in its orbit, and the solar system itself is orbiting the galaxy in a huge cycle. I mean, everything's in motion, all the time, and this is well known. Can you explain this?

No, I can't... but I know what you mean, and the portals do stay in specific locations, kind of anchored to this planet. That does happen that way. Why they don't get left behind or just kind of float off somewhere, I have no idea. Maybe they're gravitationally anchored in some way. Your guess is as good as mine. One of the portals connects to Mars, and it's a stable connection, no matter where Earth and Mars are in their orbits. We have a base there established in the early sixties. Actually, we have several bases.

So we've explored Mars already.

Sure, a long time ago. Have you seen *Alternative Three*?

Yes.

That had some truth to it. The Mars landing video was all a spoof, and other parts of it were as well, but there's truth there.

What else do you know as a physicist working on these projects?

OK. This may interest you if you have a physics background. You know what signal non-locality is, right? When two particles in different parts of the universe can apparently communicate with each other simultaneously, no matter what the distance. Communications devices have been made for communicating across vast distances and also locally using a methodology that's impossible to eavesdrop on because there's nothing traveling between the two devices that can be intercepted. It's impossible to crack or code break or eavesdrop because no signal travels anywhere, so there's no signal to be intercepted or decoded. It just doesn't work like that. The beauty of it is that the devices are actually so simple to build. You can create two chaotic circuits, on a couple of small breadboards using cheap components which anyone can buy, and they communicate with each other in this way. You can build these if you know how.

235

Are there any other applications besides communication?

[pause]Yes.

What else can you tell us about this?

That's it. Oh, I should say that I didn't realize at first that you were also the guy who created the Serpo website. Let me just say that it wasn't called by that name. And I doubt that the travel took nine months. That's not how they traveled there.

Oh, you mean the travel was instantaneous?

[pause]I don't think they traveled the way they say they did on the Serpo website. Maybe there were other programs. There may have been many. But travel across large distances is best done using portals. Anything else is really... it's just inefficient.

You mean they used Stargates?

I guess you could call them that, yes. I also suspect the system isn't Zeta Reticuli. It sounds to me like Alpha Centauri. I think you mentioned this on the site.

Do you have a reason for saying that?

Well, Zeta 1 and 2 are a long way apart from one another. Alpha Centauri and Promixa Centauri are close together. Alpha Centauri has a solar system very much like ours, but it's older. The planets are in stable orbits. There are three inhabited planets, the second, third and fourth. No, wait, the fifth, I think. Second, third and fifth.

That's astonishing... you knew this professionally? I mean, you came across this in the course of your work?

Yes. This is known. It's comparatively easy to get there, less than five light-years away, and that's, you know, it's right next door to us. The... people... there are very human-like. They're not Grays, they're like us. The human form is very common in the universe.

[Bill] Is one of the planets desert-like? That's what I saw in the photo I described. Two setting suns, over a desert landscape. It really blew me away. [See this article on the Serpo website]

Yes, it is. A desert planet.

Wow. Are you familiar with Project Looking Glass?

That sounds kind of familiar...

It was a kind of technology that Dan Burisch told us about that involved seeing into the future. Were you involved with it?

OK, that technology wasn't developed by us. We were given it, or it was taken from a craft we acquired. I didn't work on that.

We heard they have a man-made Stargate at Los Alamos. Are you familiar with that?

[looks at us without answering, slight enigmatic smile]

What can you tell us about Los Alamos?

There's a Los Alamos website I'll send you, and then you can search there under "gravity shielding" and things like that. It's all there.*[Note: the website is lanl.arxiv.org.]*Now, it may have been an error that it's in the public domain. You might want to advise people to archive the pages they find there before they're taken off the web once this gets out if it does. But right now you can see it with your own eyes. It's hard to know what else to say.

What can you tell us about the ET presence?

Look up the movie *Wavelength*. It's based on a totally true story. Have you seen it? It's based on an incident that took place at Hunter Liggett. This is a hot one.

No. Where's Hunter Liggett?

90 miles south-south-east of Monterey, California. My primary station at the time was Fort Ord.I was working there back in the early 70s when I was in the military, and I was working under CDCEC, which is Combat Developments Command Experimentation Command. You can go look that up. We were doing testing of all kinds of devices, and we lived out in the field there. We wore laser protection goggles a lot of the time and we had our eyes dilated routinely to check our retinas for burns. Some of the cattle in the

fields even wore modified goggles! This was the most bizarre sight you could ever imagine. Well, one day something happened while we were testing. A disk came into the area and it was hovering, it hovered right directly in front of us, out in a field. So [pause] we shot the ****ing thing down.

You shot down a disk?

[shaking head] We should never have done it. It wasn't me personally, but the group did. Between us, we had all this gizmo weaponry and I guess they panicked and thought they were in a movie or something. The disk was disabled and it was captured, and so were the occupants, and I saw these very briefly. They were small child-like humanoids, with no hair. And they had small eyes, not large almond-shaped eyes. I don't think anyone knows about this. As far as I know, it's not on the internet.

239

This is incredible. I've never heard of this incident.

Most of the other witnesses ended up in Vietnam and many were killed. I may be the only living witness to what happened... I don't know. The rest of the story is in a sci-fi movie called *Wavelength*, which was released in the early '80s. I'd never heard of it until I ran into it years later, in Arizona. Did I just say this? [laughs, for the first time]When I saw the video, I was expecting some, you know, light entertainment with a beer or two, but I mean, my mouth just hung wide open.

The beginning of the film just completely clearly and accurately describes the incident, and the film is very close to the rest of the story, including the use of an abandoned Nike base in Southern California to store them. Go find it. It's all true. I was just amazed when I saw it. The person who wrote it must have been there or knew someone who was there. But I don't know who. I had a genuine alien photo once. I showed it to someone, a woman, a very talented woman, who was a microbiologist working for one of the agencies. It scared the s*** out of her. I couldn't believe it. She just didn't want to deal with it at all. And I'd say that just suggests that the public, even scientists aren't ready for this information to be released. And this person was really smart. It didn't stop her from freaking out, just not wanting to know. She was just, you know, totally spooked.

240

Do you still have the photo? Can we see it?

I don't know. I may still have it somewhere, and if I can find it, I'll forward it to you.

Can you describe it?

It showed a small being with dark skin, kind of black and wrinkled. He was a sole survivor of an incident. But he died shortly afterwards. He had a suit that was self-healing, ah... self-repairing. It was a kind of fabric or something, that would repair itself. And he had an artifact with him that was some kind of remote control device, and that was taken away from him.

He was the survivor of a crash?

[pause]No.

A time traveler?

You know everything, don't you?

No, but you're giving us verification.

I mean, it's just so incredibly complicated. It's so complex it's possible that no one person has all the information. Most of the agencies don't know what the other agencies know and everything is heavily compartmentalized right up the wazoo. No-one talks to anyone else about this stuff. Sometimes entire projects are duplicated at the cost of God knows how many billions because the existence of the other project is unknown, it's kept from them. I mean, I'm a scientist, and scientists sometimes have one arm tied behind their backs because they can't communicate freely. They can't communicate at all [laughs]. And there are dozens, hundreds of classified projects, I mean major ones. It's just a total mess. Look, there are many groups of ETs, and besides our own *ancestors* are mixed in there. There are time loops upon time loops, and it's all a mess. You'd need an IQ of 190 to figure it all out.

(241)

Tell us about the time loops. By the way, can we ask you again.... you've not heard of Dan Burisch?

Not that I remember. It's not familiar to me.

We interviewed him last month. He was next to John Lear on the web page.

I did see your interview with John Lear, talking about the moon photos and the way they're airbrushed. NASA does that all the time. He's quite a character, by the way. I'd like to meet him one day. What few people know is that radar reports for the National Weather Service are also airbrushed, so that certain radar images aren't released. I don't mean airbrushed as in by hand. The radar images are electronically filtered using software. Some of these radar traces are huge. In addition, the weather radar won't record traces that are moving faster than a certain high speed, a couple of thousand miles an hour. But there are still traces which need to be removed.

UFOs?

Sure. They're often optically invisible, but usually, show up on radar. They're also visible in ultraviolet... I don't think this is generally known by people.

So what can you tell us about the time loops?

Right. [long pause]The situation with time loops is that there are a large number of parallel timelines, lots of branches. There are no paradoxes. [draws a diagram] If you go back in time and kill your grandfather, that's the grandfather paradox everyone talks about, there's no paradox. When you go back and change the past, it creates a different timeline, which is a new branch of the original one. On that timeline, you'd not be born and wouldn't exist, so that aspect of the paradox is true. Do you see? But on this timeline, which you're on here and now, you do exist and continue to do so. There's no paradox. It's simple... do you see? You're dealing with different branches of a kind of time tree. No principles get violated. All future events are possibilities, not certainties. That's kind of pretty important, an important... distinction. That's really all I can say about that.

Do you know anything about chemtrails?

OK. Chemtrails were developed by Edward Teller and are basically the seeding of thousands of tons of microparticles of aluminum on the upper atmosphere to try to increase the albedo of the planet, the reflectivity of the planet, because of global warming. Now, *gold* microparticles, real gold, were used once in a similar situation on another planet, but I guess they had lots of gold, and we used aluminum instead. Global warming is partly because of the greenhouse effect, and that certainly makes things worse, but most of it is because of increased solar activity. Solar activity is the real problem.

Why isn't this information in the public domain? It seems like people should know and would like to know, and there's no security risk if what you say is true.

243

Scientifically, it's just a total gamble. Not nearly enough is understood. It may work, or maybe it won't. It could easily make things worse. There may also be health side-effects, weather side-effects, God knows what. It affects the whole planet and here you have a unilateral, non-democratic decision, unconnected with the political or democratic process, to launch a huge technological special project that affects everyone on earth. If that's not controversial, I don't know what is. The solution is to keep it secret. It's the usual kneejerk solution, too.

Will it work?

I don't know.

Is this also connected with weather wars?

[pause]Yes, there are weather wars. The Air Force will own the weather within two years.

What else can you tell us?

Read *The Report from Iron Mountain*. Much of that is true. I was working with a group down in [_____]. They called us in and passed out a report. The weird thing is that it wasn't even connected with what we were working on, and it came just right out of the blue, out of nowhere, and none of us were expecting it. The guy said, and I'll never forget it because it struck me as just wrong: "There are the wolves and there are the sheep, and we are the wolves." Then they told us to go and read the report, and that was that.There wasn't any choice, and there still isn't. The way they see it is there are too many people, and, you know, they're right. That's true. So they figure they need to eliminate them and they're planning solutions to this. I happen to think it doesn't have to be that way. Apart from what I've mentioned so far about the spacetime problems, the problem is overpopulation. It's as simple as that. There are programs to reduce global population for everyone's benefit. Believe it or not, the intent there is positive. It was put together by Kennedy way back then. The RAND Corporation was involved, and one of the Rockefellers, I forget which one, probably Laurance, I think.

By killing people off?

Basically, yes. Artificial viruses that have been deployed using a number of means and are hard to detect or identify and nearly impossible to cure. Medical people in the public domain can't identify what's happening.

245

How do you feel about this personally?

Very mixed. [pause]As an individual flesh-and-blood human being, I'm appalled. And as a scientist trained to look at things from a high vantage point, a high overview, I have to say that I can understand the thinking. You have to understand that I'm not defending or condoning this. It's just a comment from an abstract scientific perspective. But the problems we face on this planet are so huge that very few people have the training or experience to view it all, to see it all in the same field of vision. My situation was different, and I got a chance to see a lot of things because of the nature of my work. Most people don't see it all. But I've worked with many agencies, and I have the big picture. Do you know that it's legal to test biological and chemical agents against US citizens? It's *legal*. You know, all that has to be done is to get the approval of the mayor of the city, or his equivalent in any area. Or some representative official. No-one knows this, but it can be checked out. Go look it up. It's all carefully hidden away in the law somewhere, but it's all in the public domain. It's all there.

You've revealed a whole lot of extraordinary material here in our conversation. What's the most important message you'd like to leave people with?

Look, I don't want to shock anyone, but I'm not optimistic. The problems facing us as a race on this planet are *huge*. I don't believe most civilians are ready and able to comprehend and deal with the sheer scale and complexity of it all. They have enough trouble managing their everyday lives, and these problems are on a completely different level. Overpopulation is the biggest issue. Everything else facing us is connected with this. You see, I can understand the military taking matters into their own hands. If there was full disclosure of all the problems and all the proposed solutions, do you think it would help any of us? I suggest the answer is probably not. It would just complicate matters further. But deep down

I *do* feel that everyone should know these things, or else I would not be talking with you. The essential message I want to leave with is that I do hope and want to believe that we as a people can handle all this, but sometimes I wake up in the morning and doubt it, but deep down I want people to know the important things that have been kept from us all. But sometimes I do wonder. You don't know what I haven't told you.

On 27 September, three weeks after the initial meetings, and after we had strongly urged him to view the three-part Dan Burisch video interview on the Project Camelot website, we received the following e-mail. It is quoted verbatim and in its entirety.

Dan Burisch is telling the whole truth.

I confirm this, timelines and all

Best wishes

6 October 2006.[57]

---

57 http://projectcamelotportal.com/2013/02/17/henry-deacon-aka-arthur-neumann-all-interviews-3/ accessed April 25th 2020 @18:54

APPENDIX 2

What really happened to Madeleine McCann?

10 key reasons which suggest that she was not abducted

Madeleine McCann was reported missing by her mother, Dr Kate McCann, at 10pm on Thursday 3rd May 2007. Since then, Madeleine, who was then nearly four, has become the best-known 'missing child' in the world. The McCanns' claimed she was abducted, by an abductor who has never been traced. They said they were wining and dining in a Tapas bar 100 yards away from where they had left their three young children in their holiday apartment in Praia da Luz, on the beautiful Algarve coast.

The Portuguese police believed the McCanns were involved in the disappearance of Madeleine. They were made official suspects on 7 September 2007 - and remained so until July 2008. Then, the Portuguese Attorney-General announced that there was insufficient evidence for any person to be charged in connection with Madeleine's 'disappearance', though he added that there was evidence that Madeleine was dead. The McCanns' spokesman, Clarence Mitchell, who used to head the government's 40-strong Media Monitoring Unit, whose function Mr Mitchell said was 'to control what comes out in the media', claimed that the McCanns had been 'cleared'.

In October 2007, the senior detective in charge, Goncalo Amaral, was replaced, claiming British government interference in his investigation. A few years earlier, he solved another 'missing child' case – that of 8-year-old Joana Cipriano. Her mother and uncle were convicted for her murder, having initially claimed she was abducted. Goncalo Amaral has since written a book, 'The Truth About A Lie', showing that Madeleine died in Praia da Luz. A documentary he made about Madeleine's death can be seen on YouTube, here: http://www.youtube.com/watch?v=UxGhlYTNisw

This leaflet gives 10 key reasons which suggest Madeleine was not abducted. It is a shortened version of a 64-page booklet published in Britain in December 2008, titled: "What Really Happened to Madeleine McCann? – 60 Reasons which suggest she was not abducted". Information on how to obtain this booklet is on the back of our leaflet.

Reason 1: Statistics show that the vast majority of young children reported abducted from their homes are already dead

Time after time, when young children die or are killed in their own homes, parents claim their child has really been abducted. The death may be from an accident, negligence, neglect, or deliberate act. We can simply say: young children are almost never kidnapped from inside their own homes. The Portuguese police were bound to be suspicious of the parents' claims that Madeleine had been abducted. But these statistics, though very persuasive, do not prove anything. So let us look at nine other reasons which suggest that she was not abducted.

Reason 2: The world-renowned British sniffer dogs, Eddie and Keela, detected the scent of a corpse in 10 places which strongly suggested Madeleine died in the McCanns' holiday apartment

Here are the main facts about the findings of the two British springer spaniels, Eddie and Keela:

251

- they were trained by expert dog-handler Martin Grime and are internationally famed for being able to detect the presence of a corpse (Eddie) or blood (Keela)
- Grime said that Eddie had never ever given a 'false alert' in 200 previous outings
- Eddie alerts only to human cadaverine - the scent of a human corpse. This is usually only produced in a corpse when the body has been dead for over 2 hours

- Eddie alerted to the scent of a corpse in the following places: the living room, the McCanns' bedroom, the veranda and the garden of their holiday apartment, on two of Dr Kate McCann's clothes, on a T-shirt belonging to Madeleine or brother Sean, and on the pink soft toy, 'Cuddle Cat' (despite the fact that Dr Kate McCann had already washed Cuddle Cat at least once)
- Eddie also detected the smell of death in the McCanns' hired Renault Scenic car
- Keela found blood at some of the same locations
- Eddie and Keela were taken to many other apartments and cars in Praia da Luz, but did not alert anywhere else
- checks were made by the Portuguese police as to whether anyone else had died in the McCanns' apartment or in their car. No-one had
- a neighbour made a witness statement saying that for weeks she saw the McCanns' hired car with its boot open all night long.

The dogs' evidence was therefore very clear: a corpse had been in all those 10 locations, and it could only have been the corpse of Madeleine McCann.

Reason 3: The strange reactions of the McCanns when they became aware of the sniffer dogs' findings

The McCanns initially reacted by desperately inventing possible explanations for the dogs' findings. Family members claimed the death smell on Dr Kate

McCann's clothes was due to having attended six corpses at work during the fortnight before her holiday. She even claimed that the death smell on 'Cuddle Cat' was because she took Madeleine's toy to work. Then they claimed the smell of death and body fluids found in the car could have come from 'rotting meat' and 'dirty nappies' in the boot. Finally, they fell back on claiming the dogs' findings were 'unreliable' and 'valueless'. These explanations were offered only to the media, not to the police.

Reason 4: The sheer impossibility of the abduction scenario

The McCanns have claimed that the abductor entered through an unlocked patio door, found Madeleine in the dark, then decided to open curtains, window and shutter of the children's bedroom and climb through a window 3 feet above the ground and barely 2 feet wide. He is supposed to have done this without waking any of the three children. According to the McCanns and their friends, he must have done this within the space of 2-3 minutes, in the dark, without being seen or heard, nor leaving any forensic traces like fingerprints, hair, fibres, skin fragments, shoe prints, or glove marks, nor any trace of abrasion marks on or around the window and window-sill. This scenario is so unlikely that we can simply say: this did not happen. When the window-frame was examined, only Dr Kate McCann's fingerprints were found on it.

Reason 5: The refusal of the McCanns and their friends to help the police

- in September 2007, the police asked Dr Kate McCann 48 questions about Madeleine's disappearance. She only answered this one: "Are you aware that in not answering the questions, you are jeopardising the investigation, which seeks to discover what happened to your daughter?" She answered: "Yes, if that's what the investigation thinks".
- the McCanns deleted mobile 'phone records, and refused to allow the Portuguese police to examine any of their medical or financial records including credit card records.
- the McCanns publicly offered to take a lie detector test, then changed their minds
- the McCanns and their 'Tapas 7' friends also refused to attend a proposed police reconstruction of the events the night Madeleine was reported missing. Yet they travelled to Portugal for a Channel 4 film which reconstructed their own version of what happened the night Madeleine was reported missing
- a Portuguese newspaper, *Sol*, tried to talk to one of the McCanns' friends, Dr David Payne, about what had happened. He refused to talk, saying: "This is our matter. We have a pact". He added that all requests for quotes and interviews must go through Dr Gerald McCann. Why would the group need to have what has been called a 'Pact of

Silence' about the circumstances surrounding Madeleine's 'disappearance'?

Reason 6: Changes of story by the McCanns and their friends

There have been many changes of story by the McCanns and their friends, and many contradictions within their versions of events – far too many to list here. For example:

- initially, the McCanns claimed that an abductor forced entry to the apartment by 'jemmying open the shutters'. The police and Mark Warners' staff examined the shutters, proving this was untrue. The McCanns quickly changed their story to say the abductor must have come in via the open patio door and exited through a small bedroom window
- the description of an abductor by McCanns' friend Jane Tanner changed several times
- until very recently, the McCanns' website described a moustachioed man, over 6ft tall, as 'the probable abductor', when there was no evidence connecting this man, seen by a tourist days before Madeleine was reported missing, to the events the night Madeleine went missing. Further, he looks nothing like the 5' 7" man described by Jane Tanner.

Reason 7: The McCanns' rush to appoint lawyers and PR experts

Immediately Madeleine was reported missing, the McCanns appointed many lawyers and public relations experts to help them, including extradition lawyers. What use would lawyers and PR experts be in finding their daughter? Maybe the McCanns knew from the outset that they would need lawyers and PR folk to defend them?

Reason 8: The strange reactions of the McCanns and their friends after she claimed to have found Madeleine missing

What is one to make of these reactions of Dr Kate McCann on finding Madeleine missing and stating she noticed the shutter and window open?

- she searched the apartment 'for 10 minutes', despite on her own evidence the probability that she was not there
- she left the twins in her apartment whilst she ran to the 'Tapas Bar' to raise the alarm
- she failed to check on the twins' well-being. The first thought through most mothers' minds would have been whether they could also have been interfered with.

In addition:

- in the days after Madeleine went missing, the McCanns were apparently happy to leave the twins in the crèche whilst they courted the media. If they were genuinely distraught by losing one child, would they not stay protectively close to the two they had left?

- the McCanns admit they never physically searched for Madeleine
- despite the claim of Jane Tanner that she had seen a man walking with a child in a certain direction, the McCanns and their friends failed to organise a concerted search in along the route he might have taken.

Reason 9: Making long-term plans to mark Madeleine's alleged abduction - whilst claiming she was alive and could still be found

From the early days, the McCanns made plans for events to mark the day Madeleine went missing - a sign they did not expect to find her:

- just a month after she 'disappeared', Dr Gerald McCann said: "We want a big event to raise awareness that she is still missing. It won't be a one-year anniversary, it will be sooner than that"
- then, on 28 June 2007, he said: "I have no doubt we will be able to sustain a high profile for Madeleine's disappearance in the long-term"
- the McCanns trade-marked the name 'Madeleine's Fund' and highlighted Madeleine's eye defect - the coloboma - boasting that her eye defect was 'a valuable marketing ploy'. This was against the advice of the Portuguese police. You can view

where Dr Gerald McCann says this at:
http://www.youtube.com/watch?v=SvdnzIGtf50

Why make long-term plans if Madeleine could be
found at any time? Strangely, Madeleine's eye defect
does not figure in 'Missing Person' descriptions of her
on the Portuguese police or Interpol websites. In
March 2009, before a Parliamentary Committee, Dr
McCann claimed British media made Madeleine 'a
commodity'. Yet just a fortnight after Madeleine went
missing, he and his advisors set up a website, a
private company to raise money (note: not a charity),
and produced goods for sale.

Reason 10: Dr Kate McCann washing the toy 'Cuddle
Cat'

The McCanns claimed Madeleine always took her
favourite soft toy, 'Cuddle Cat', with her. They then
said the abductor had handled 'Cuddle Cat', placing it
on 'a high shelf or ledge'. The abductor could have left
valuable forensic traces on the toy. So why did Dr Kate
McCann decide to thoroughly wash it, something most
mothers say they could never do to the soft toy of
their missing child. Later, despite Dr Kate McCann
washing Cuddle Cat, cadaver dog Eddie detected the
smell of death on it. The smell of death remains on
items long after they have been thoroughly cleaned.

WHAT YOU CAN DO NOW

If Madeleine McCann was not abducted, and died in the McCanns' apartment in Portugal, as the original senior detective in the case has very good reason to believe, then those that caused or allowed her death have - so far - got away with it. To read more about what really happened to Madeleine McCann, you can order "What Really Happened to Madeleine McCann? - 60 reasons which suggest she was not abducted" from our website: www.madeleinefoundation.org or from the address below. Or visit one of these three websites which also have further information:

www.mccannfiles.com   www.truthformadeleine.com www.the3arguidos.net

To join our campaign for justice for Madeleine McCann, contact The Madeleine Foundation,   66 Chippingfield, HARLOW, Essex, CM17 0DJ Tel: 01279 635789 e-mail: ajsbennett@btinternet.com website: www.madelelinefoundation.org

Second edition published and printed by Supporters of The Madeleine Foundation, 15 August 2009

Read This First! Download

Why I Know That You Do Not Love Your Children! Ebook FREE!

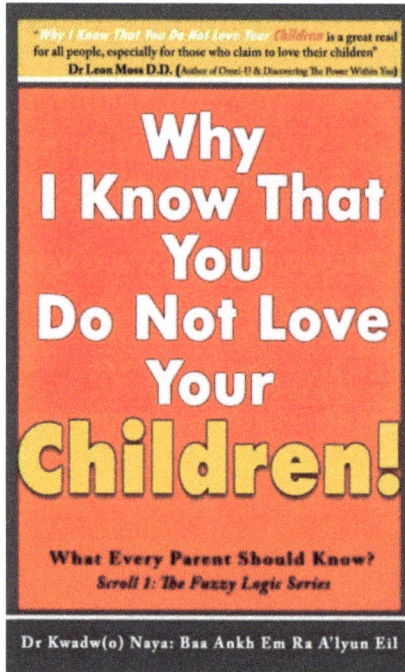

Just to say thanks for reading my book, I would like to give you a free e-book! ($6.99 Value)

https://BookHip.com/JFWKZB

PLEASE LOOK OUT FOR CHOICES 2

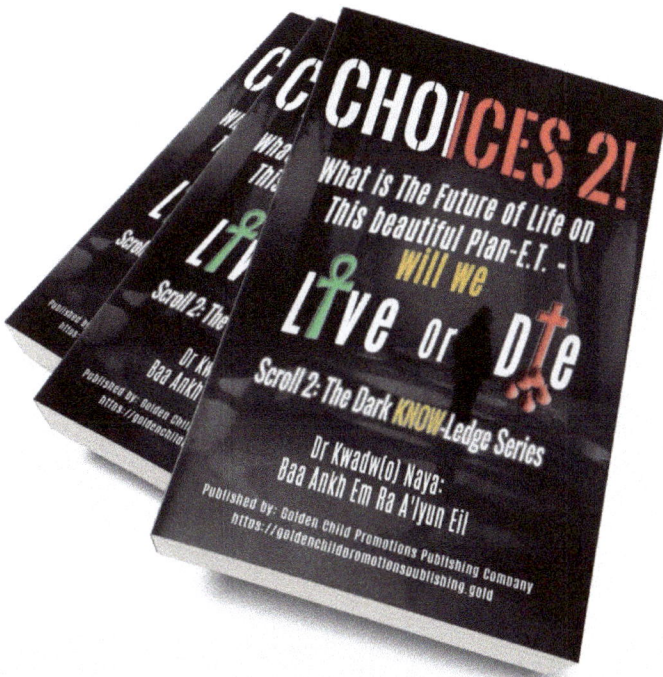

You can pre-order your own copy for only $1.30 here on Amazon (for a limited period only):

https://www.amazon.com/dp/B084611YYT?ref_=pe_3052
080_276849420

ABOUT

THE AUTHOR

Kwadw(o) Naya: Baa Ankh Em Ra A'lyun Eil

Born: Catterick Garrison, UK

Nationality: British

Race: Carbonite (Autochthonous)

Genre: Non-Fiction

Notable awards: PHD in Life and a master's in business as well as many other vocational qualifications.

Kwadw(o) Naya: Baa Ankh Em Ra A'lyun Eil is an Author, Director, Mentor and Life Coach ('Transformational'), he is a new gentleman on the scene, one of the most promising newcomers for 2019.

He was born in a country where he has never been accepted, raised in a broken poverty-stricken home, which he was thrown out at the age of 15 never to return. Surprisingly he has had a very good career,

NOT GREAT, and is educated to master's level with 'degrees' in street knowledge. Despite his successes there has always been some unseen FORCES working against him, which he is only too happy to share.

Somehow, he has excelled with everything that he has touched and is not afraid of CHANGE, moving from running his own estate agency in the capital city of London (UK) to becoming a fully established author, mentor and life coach.

Kwadw(o) Naya: Baa Ankh Em Ra A'lyun Eil is ready to share his KNOWLEDGE, WISDOM, and OVERSTANDING with YOU ALL.

He has now written 25 books to date.